GEOFF GORSUCH

ON EAGLES' WINGS

NAVPRESS

A MINISTRY OF THE NAVIGATORS
P.O. BOX 6000, COLORADO SPRINGS, COLORADO 80934

The Navigators is an international Christian organization. Jesus Christ gave His followers the Great Commission to go and make disciples (Matthew 28:19). The aim of The Navigators is to help fulfill that commission by multiplying laborers for Christ in every nation.

NavPress is the publishing ministry of The Navigators. NavPress publications are tools to help Christians grow. Although publications alone cannot make disciples or change lives, they can help believers learn biblical discipleship, and apply what they learn to their lives and ministries.

© 1989 by Geoffrey Gorsuch
All rights reserved, including translation
Library of Congress Catalog Card Number:
  88-63388
ISBN 08910-92625

Cover art: An OV-10 Bronco by Gary Meyer

All Scripture quotations in this publication are from the *Holy Bible: New International Version* (NIV). Copyright © 1973, 1978, 1984, International Bible Society. Used by permission of Zondervan Bible Publishers.

Printed in the United States of America

CONTENTS

To my father and mother,
Clifford and Helen Gorsuch,
who gave me the greatest gift anyone can have
in preparation for the rigors of life:
their love.
In my youth they disciplined me,
in the early years of my manhood
they counseled and encouraged me,
and now, in the summer of my life,
they have granted me
the privilege of their friendship.

I've heard it said that
if any generation can see just a little farther,
it's only because they're standing
on the shoulders of giants.
From my perspective, that says it all,
and leaves me reduced to a simple but heartfelt
"thank you."

AUTHOR

Geoffrey Gorsuch is a Navigator representative in Strasbourg, France. He and his wife, Diane, have served with The Navigators also at the Air Force Academy in Colorado Springs, at the University of Colorado in Boulder, and in Grenoble, France.

Geoff spent eighteen months in Vietnam as a pilot of an OV-10 Bronco, a light-strike reconnaissance aircraft. He served as a "FAC," a Forward Air Controller, controlling all air activities in an assigned sector. As a United States Air Force pilot, Geoff reached the rank of captain, and received the Silver Star, four Distinguished Flying Crosses, twelve Air Medals, and the Vietnamese Cross of Gallantry.

FOREWORD

I met Geoff Gorsuch the day after he met Christ. He had listened to Dr. Bob Smith of Bethel College give a message to Air Force Academy cadets on the subject "How to Be a Successful Failure"—the person who has it all, yet knows deep in his soul that he has nothing. After the message, Geoff told Ken Brothers, a fellow cadet, that he wanted to establish the kind of living relationship with God that Dr. Bob had talked about. Ken, a dedicated Christian, led Geoff to Christ. And he told him about a group of Christians known as The Navigators who could help him grow in a day-by-day deeper fellowship with the Lord. The next day Geoff was sitting on my front porch—full of excitement, full of questions, and full of zeal to serve his newfound Savior.

This book follows Geoff's pilgrimage in his life of faith. Much of it deals with his time in Vietnam and the tough lessons he learned about himself, the Lord, and life itself. We go with him as he pilots a crippled airplane through a turbulent tropical storm, trying to find an airstrip that is socked in. We travel with him as he faces death to help in the rescue of downed comrades. We are with him as he watches a rescue helicopter go down in flames. And we continue with him as he sits in his tent, Bible in hand. There he tries, amid victories and defeats, to get the pieces to fit, searching the Scriptures for the answers he knows can be found nowhere else.

This is an exciting book. It is a soul-searching book. You will find it hard to put down. You will enter into the private world of this young warrior and listen as he silently cries out to God for answers. And as a former combat Marine in World War II, I can tell you that it is an honest book, filled with all the emotions of a man coping with fear and death. *On Eagles' Wings* is a book you will surely find helpful as you reflect on your own pilgrimage of faith.

LEROY EIMS

ACKNOWLEDGMENTS

I would like to thank Don Simpson and Kathy Yanni, who were very instrumental in helping me "get airborne." They will never know how much they ministered to my life during those early phases of the project. And I would like to thank Jon Stine, who "rendezvoused" with me, somewhat like a wingman does, to hold me to the course we had set. His calls, letters, and editing always seemed to be what I needed at the time to get through the doubts and make it to the final approach and landing. I simply could not have done it without the help of these "crewmen." I'm honored to know them.

INTRODUCTION

From behind the tree line, mortars and light mobile artillery continued to pound the Allied position in preparation for the full-scale offensive. It was the spring of '72 and the Cambodian fishing village of Pouthisat was under siege. As the Khmer Rouge pressed their attack, the beleaguered forces of the Lon Nol regime, the unofficial ally of the United States, were barely holding on. The communist forces, indoctrinated and fully confident that their ideology would in fact usher in a bold new age for Cambodia, apparently found nothing to fear in attacking this lightly fortified peasant township—except, perhaps its ally, the United States.

I had just left the runway on what I thought would be a routine reconnaissance mission in my sector. I was going through the normal post-takeoff checklist items when Lt. Chung Vaan, the leader of this small force under attack, screamed at me in French, *"Nail, Nail, Venez vite! Nous avons* besoin de vous! Ils attaquent! Vite! Vite! Venez vite!" ("Nail, Nail! [my call sign]. Come quickly! We're being overrun! Come quickly!") Never before in all our previous exchanges had I heard him cry out in such desperation.

But for the past several months, the situation in Cambodia had progressively deteriorated as the scales tipped in favor of Pol Pot's well-organized and equipped communist force. What Chung Vaan knew instinctively—that Pol Pot would prove to be the butcher of Cambodia—the rest of the world would not comprehend until it was too late. And even upon seeing the evidence, equal to the horrors uncovered at the end of WW II, the watching world could only shake its head in wonder at how such a pastoral setting of thatched villages, temples, and rice patties could be transformed into a tragic holocaust.

As with everyone else, the impact of what was happening did not fully register with me as I "did the job." As we coordinated air strikes with the Cambodian Air Force, which in this emergency had been placed in my tactical command, we sought out enemy supply lines and destroyed them. And so the siege was lifted. A grateful Chung Vaan sent a letter that eventually reached the White House. We had done the job. America had helped to buy them some time!

But it was not enough. Two years later, safely at home, I picked up the morning paper over a leisurely breakfast, looking forward to the afternoon game (a bowl bid was at stake!). There it was, in matter-of-fact black and white: Cambodia had fallen. The paper coolly reported that though there were "rumors of reprisals," there would perhaps "at long last" be peace in Cambodia. I hoped so. But I couldn't help but wonder what happened to Chung Vaan. I had been marked by his cry over the radio. From time to time I can still hear it as though it was just yesterday.

His cry would be multiplied by millions. But this time there would be no one there to hear. Not until it was too late! The truth started to trickle out—a rumor here, an eyewitness account there. As the press, in a state of shock, began to fit together the pieces of the puzzle the historians now call the "Cambodian Holocaust," I began to try to recontact through channels the young lieutenant who had fought so bravely and had been so thankful. But the communists were slaughtering Cambodia, and his continued silence confirmed my worst fears.

I couldn't help but talk about it, but nobody wanted to listen. And to this day, I don't blame them. Americans were tired of the war, and scandal on the home front had sapped what little energy remained for moral combat. So I felt alone. It now seemed much the same as it did back in the war, only this time I had time to think. Perhaps I thought too much. But as images surfaced, I found myself finally facing—psychologically digesting—what I had lived not so long ago.

Occasionally, in the midst of getting on with life, I found myself tearful and I didn't know why. Chung Vaan? Perhaps. There were times when I would experience nearly uncontrollable rage. Why? I initially thought it was a legitimate—even righteous!—anger aimed at the godless ideology that had destroyed Cambodia. And though that seemed reasonable enough, I am convinced that the explanation could only be found at a deeper, more universal level. I was in mourning—mourning the death of my innocence. The world, life in general, was just not going to conform to my expectations. The death of Chung Vaan was in many ways the death of who I was and what I had hoped mankind—"we"—could become.

You see, I was a "believer." God and country. Science and progress. Democracy. My father had kissed my mother goodbye in '41 and he didn't come home 'til '45—'til it was over! Yes sir! Can do! We won!

My youth was during the Eisenhower years of peace, prosperity, and "father knows best." Then a young president ushered in Camelot, and found a nation of baby boomers ready to respond to the challenge to "pay any price." The Peace Corps was launched and, animated by the same wave of optimism and zeal, I went off to the Air Force Academy. I was as sincere as they come—a true believer. Unfortunately, I just didn't know what kind of world was out there waiting for me.

As the Marines left for Da Nang, an assassin's bullet shattered Camelot. Reality. A reality that I refused. For even though Jesus Himself had said there would be wars and rumors of wars, kings against kings, nations against nations, famines, earthquakes, and the betrayal of humanity on a monumental scale, I didn't believe Him! I refused to believe Him! And even though Solomon in all his regal splendor and wisdom had said that mankind lives, generation after generation, for that which leads only to frustration and ultimately to despair and death, I didn't believe him! And just as the prophets of the Old Testament warned time and time again that God will judge the motives and actions of men and nations by exposing them for the vain, fleeting gestures they really are, I said to myself, "Ah, c'mon. God's not like that! He's one of the good guys."

You see, I was a believer—but I was not a learner. My utopian expectations for myself, my fellow man, and the systems we would resourcefully devise were still intact. What I didn't like about the Bible, other than the way some people handled it, was that it "tells it like it is."

It took a chaotic war and its tragic aftermath to make me a person who could learn from life and its Author. Like those Marines coming home from Da Nang, I was no longer a man in the springtime of life, even though my body was still young. As one veteran put it, we were old heads on young shoulders. But through my wartime experience and the years since then, I have found, with the much needed help of many mature men who have come to the same impasse in life, that the God of comfort is also the God of confrontation. He's the "jealous" God who wants the best of us. Through His sovereign power He will arrange the circumstances of our lives, at times painfully, if necessary, to bring that to pass. The key is learning—seeing life as an encounter with the divine and responding properly. A disciple is a learner because he has to be.

It is always dangerous to say that you have learned something. The apostle Paul teaches us that at best we see through a glass darkly. But let me say that I *am* learning, struggling to get on with meaningful living in the midst of, and often in spite of, hard-core reality. I went over to Vietnam living in light of the vicissitudes of this world, but I came back living in light of eternity.

The principles I've discovered in my own spiritual odyssey, primarily from Paul's teaching in the book of Romans, have changed my life. Over the years, I've had the privilege of sharing them with people around our troubled world. Their response encourages me to continue. It's in this spirit that I now take pen in hand. The stories I tell are from those experiences closest to me and are told only to illustrate, not to justify, any "position" held during the turbulent Vietnam era.

Part of learning, you see, is forgiveness.

CHAPTER ONE

Where Is God?

"If I go to the east, [God] is not there; if I go to the
west, I do not find him. When he is at work in the
north, I do not see him; when he turns to the south,
I catch no glimpse of him."
(Job 23:8-9)

■

It was the "winter" of '71, 88° in the shade. As an armed reconnaissance pilot seeking out "targets of opportunity," I was flying toward one of many fortified villages dotting the Cambodian countryside. Protected by a mix of concertina wire and earthen revetments, this assortment of thatched dwellings and government buildings of stucco and sheet metal represented home for a few thousand stoic Buddhist people. They had known nothing but war for many generations. Though the warriors' flags periodically changed, the actual battlefield, their homeland, hadn't.

Somehow—God only knows how!—I found myself with many others from my generation, an ocean away from home. Though many of us believed in "the American dream," we now found ourselves profoundly questioning its meaning. It was the Vietnam era.

I had just received orders over "the radios" to see if

there was any unusual activity in this area that was normally considered to be safe—"pacified." As smoke greeted me on the horizon, the kind of smoke I had already seen too many times before, I cursed myself for having arrived too late. The village, just a fishing community nestled on the Tonle Sap, was in flames. I applied full power to the plane and armed my rockets and machine guns for any eventuality. However, I was shocked to discover that the situation was not what I had anticipated. It was not the communists that were destroying the village. A Cambodian gunboat commander—our *ally*—was shelling his own people!

All of our previous information indicated that this area was solidly loyal to the government—and us. In my mind's eye, I began to review the most recent intelligence reports that could in some way shed light on this tragic situation. But there were none! How could this be happening? Why would the government attack the "friendlies"? I got on the radios in an effort to contact our squadron headquarters, intelligence centers, and ultimately the American Embassy in Pnom Penh. As I described the carnage taking place just a few thousand feet below me, even the ambassador, who had direct operational control over any commitments American air forces made in Cambodia, could not understand it.

A horrible mistake was being made. There was simply no information available that would adequately explain what appeared to be nothing short of wanton destruction. Then, with all my options exhausted, I slipped into the despairing realization that I had accidentally become the witness to something I had only heard about in previous briefings: the tribal feuds.

Bad blood between tribes and clans—each speaking its own dialect, its people worshiping their own ancestors and loyal to their own chief—had gone on way before Western attempts to baptize and democratize the region. But although the ways of the West were rejected, its arms weren't. And, to our great regret, at times those arms were used to further the age-old tribal fratricide rather than to stop the impending communist-led genocide. Apparently this was one of those times.

Circling over the destroyed crops and the village, which were burning to a charred ruin, I looked down on the inhabitants, mainly the women and children whom the military conscription had overlooked. They were now left to wander and perhaps die. I was suddenly struck by the fact that this was Christmas Day. "Merry Christmas, world! Merry damn Christmas!" I muttered to myself in tear-filled anger, choking on the realization that I was powerless to stop it. "The suffering . . . Oh, God . . . Where are You?"

My thoughts were riveted to the horrifying realities of my duties as the radios spoke over the roar of my engines and my personal rage. The military attaché at the embassy routinely ordered me to stay in the area until "bingo" in order to prepare a full report. Bingo—minimum fuel needed to safely return to base. As I looked at the fuel gauges and quickly calculated how much my turboprop jet engines would need, I realized that I had just been ordered to stand by and helplessly watch for two more hours! Duty.

But, what exactly *were* my duties in this confused war? It seemed the more I saw, the less I understood. And worse, even though I was a Christian, I had begun to question the basic goodness of God. Too many months in the theater of war had begun to take its toll on me. In the midst of the life-and-death struggle and all its ambiguity, mere survival seemed to be the unspoken order of the day. Just get home! Emotionally, I had begun to vacillate somewhere between anger and despair. I cared. I didn't. I wanted to win. I couldn't. At times I even questioned my own sanity as my mind, schooled in "the American dream," was forced to face up to this unremitting nightmare. But I wasn't the only one.

I remember well another young pilot stressed out by the round-the-clock flying and the intensity of the antiaircraft fire. He stood up one morning during breakfast and shouted out, "We're killing people! We're killing people! We're killing people!" With his long-tormented soul bared before his colleagues and his desperate need written all over his prematurely aged face, his eyes pleaded for some sort of rhyme or reason for it all. Standing there, dumb, his confused silence shouted the unspoken question on the heart of every man: Where was God in this mess? Where in the world was He?!

Eternal seconds passed. Then the silence was finally shattered by a grizzled veteran who, mustering all the compassion he possibly could, said, "Shut up and sit down, Socrates. Welcome to the world!" As he slowly sat down, lowering his head into his hands to hide his shame and tears, the only slightly ruffled audience went back to their bacon and eggs . . . and eventually, the war.

Later, as he and I talked, the subject of God occasionally surfaced, only to be submerged again in his personal tidal wave of unanswered questions. Why? He wanted to believe, but—he just couldn't. How could a loving God permit what he had seen—and done? And so on. For him, life to this point had been relatively easy: middle class America, TV, college, girls, and jets. And, like many, he had even learned how to wash away the ill effects of the war with a good stiff drink or two in the "pay as you go" company of a woman.

But now he demanded answers. He demanded to know *why*. Or, more specifically, "Why *me*?" All the explanations he had ever heard were simply no longer big enough to encompass the reality he was facing. And though we were all brought time and again to the point of asking *why*, the question haunted him till he began to babble almost incoherently. Mercifully, his tour of duty was terminated early and he was sent home to receive professional care. Yes, occasionally mercy could still be found. And there was also grace. However, most just called it luck.

But whatever it was, eventually we, the survivors—there were no victors over there—began to feel alien to this world. It was as though someone had granted us some sort of borrowed time to explore the heights, depths, and mystery of life itself. And most of us just didn't know who that someone was. As the months passed, our squadron and sister squadrons sustained some heavy losses. Though some of the pilots had been rescued, "patched up," and sent home, others less fortunate had been captured and marched off in bare feet to the "Hanoi Hilton."

As P.O.W. became a household term in America, still other men I had personally known were never heard from again. M.I.A. is probably their epitaph. And for what, I asked? Just another "damned" Christmas? The embittered cynic's "welcome to the world"? Or, was there something of the divine in this life? Someone we could turn to when life moved beyond our capacity to make sense out of it?

No one escapes!
It was a world full of despair. But I wasn't yet to the point of thinking that life was void of meaning or true happiness, though many others were. After all, the "pursuit of happiness" was the essence of the American dream. I'd certainly reached out for my share. Often I sat back and reflected on all those joys: Taking the final shot at the hoop to win the championship game. My first love. The first kiss. Thanksgiving. Family. And other more rational Christmas seasons with nothing more on my mind than guessing what the outcome of the bowl games would be. "Middle-class America." In the midst of the frustration of the war, I often sought refuge in

those memories, the pleasant times. And I was thankful—to God, my parents, and my country.

And yet, for all of us, there are those other times when we feel soiled, if not outraged, by our world. Life! And though on a daily basis the newspapers reveal monumental betrayal of trust, heartache, and suffering, we're never quite so moved as when it hits home: in our city, our neighborhood, or our own family. Only then will we own it—or own up to it. "Our" world. At those times, how do we explain *why* when the illusions of life give way to sheer pain? We cry out, "Where's the justice? Where's God? Why is this happening? Why me? . . ."

With our eyes veiled in tears and our hands outstretched, we look toward heaven expecting something . . . a blessing . . . an answer. And we wait. And we wait. And as time passes, our anger and frustration mount and we ever-so-slowly close those prayerful hands into gnarled, clenched fists, and with our anger now focused on God, we shake them at heaven, demanding an answer.

And we're met with silence. And more silence. Is anyone there?!

And, as it was with Job, even our friends don't know what to say. We feel alone. Profoundly alone and vulnerable. And, perhaps for the first time in our lives, we're frightened. And answerless. And so it goes. On, and on, and on.

Though with time the mind mercifully forgets, the scars remain and life is irrevocably changed. We "see" things differently. But how differently depends on the unique response of the individual, what we choose to learn from it. It seems as though it's not a question of *if* life-changing circumstances will happen to each and every one of us. It's only *when*. As the apostle says, "No temptation [test] has seized you except what is common to man . . . ." Mine was Vietnam.

Other wars

As I finally descended the stairs of the "freedom flight" that had brought me home safe and sound, I was met by some old friends and the sudden overwhelming realization that I could not turn back the clock. I had changed. Only, I didn't yet know why or how. Everything was the same. Yet everything was so different. There we stood, me in my summer tan uniform, they in theirs—cut-offs, sweat shirts, and Adidas.

After some slightly awkward small talk (what do you say to a guy who's been in a war?), we finally got around to talking about other wars and other battles. A mutual friend was now fighting for his life against cancer. Whether he would make it through the year was doubtful. He and his family had befriended me at a time when I really needed a helping hand—someone who would listen, understand. I knew that he would be greatly missed and that the world would somehow seem just a little more lonely without him. So I whispered, "Why? . . . Oh, God, why? . . . Where are You?" I wondered about his family—how they were going to handle it. And so on.

As we sat there waiting for my luggage, the silence of my thoughts was interrupted by some more small talk. The Super Bowl. The world series. Fads and trends and a little light Americana . . . till we got on the subject of divorce— American style. I learned of another friend of mine who was trying to pick up the pieces of his broken marriage. In many ways they had been the model couple. Ten happy years. "Oh, God, what happened?" So we talked about what they were experiencing. Feelings of failure. Fear of the future. I openly wondered if they would ever be able to find happiness again. No one could say. Apparently, one of the estranged partners no longer "gave a damn." And what about the children? Their lovely home? And so the conversation went . . . till there was nothing more to say.

As we threw my bags into the "van" (something America had discovered during my absence) we awkwardly returned to the safer ground of small talk. Cars. Girls. An anecdote here, memory there. Then someone mentioned the old beer softball games of our more carefree youth. Sun and fun! There was laughter as we slipped into the old macho one-upmanship that so typifies young American men groping for deeper communication. As we drove off, someone mentioned hamburgers.

Having never been to a "Humpty Dumpty" hamburger stand, I wasn't quite ready for what happened when we drove in. Humpty Dumpty himself danced out to our car, stuck his head into the window of the passenger side where I was sitting, and seeing my uniform and officer's insignia, he said, "Hi, soldier boy. Did you shoot your gun today?" With that, something inside of me snapped. Something screamed that I wasn't yet ready for America—and probably America wasn't ready for me. We both needed some more time.

Somewhere between commanding and asking, I strongly suggested that Humpty Dumpty move on . . . and so should we. "ASAP!" Everyone complied. However, a few miles, burgers, and fries later, the awkward silence was broken by the radio as the DJ began to play the "oldies but goodies." After a while, the conversation was relaxed . . . safe. But try as we did to keep it light, we couldn't. With the arrival of the news broadcast and the commentary it inspired, reality just kept crashing into the conversation like an uninvited guest leaving us silent before the unanswered question. Where was God in all the sickness, bankruptcy, betrayal, lay-offs—and pain?

A bigger answer

I was not yet ready to talk about my own experiences. But as I listened to the others, I found myself quietly understanding just how tough it could be. For some strange reason I had been thinking that I was all alone. That everyone else was having it better. Or easier. As we all do, I had somehow thought that my own personal experience was the only way to be brought to the point of needing a "bigger answer." Of profoundly wondering about the nature of God. If He was supposed to be so good and so much in control . . . why? Where was He?

After watching that village burn to the ground that fateful Christmas day, I had slowly walked back to my Quonset hut with a simple childlike prayer on my lips: "Oh, God, where are You?" Numbed and almost in a trance, I had prayed over and over again, "Show me sanity. . . . Show me Your hand in all this." Given the circumstances, it was the only logical prayer left to me. Its motivation was not so much a self-flattering personal piety as it was the growing fear of the cynical despair that seemed to be the "answer" of the prayerless. Indifference—the world's counterfeit of God's promised peace. There just had to be more than "Shut up and sit down, Socrates. . . . " I was fighting for my life.

I had been so sure. We all had. But now we were facing the frustration of not knowing. We had leaned too heavily on past perspectives and found them inadequate for facing the future. However, this sense of loss prepared me for the words of an Old Testament prophet who had spoken to his people, whose dreams had also been shattered: "Even youths grow tired and weary, and young men stumble and fall; but those who hope in the LORD will renew their strength. They will soar on wings like eagles; they will run and not grow weary, they will walk and not be faint" (Isaiah 40:30-31).

I was only twenty-five. Yet I felt so old. Tired. I was in shape . . . we had to be! I hadn't gained a pound since graduation. Yet something was weighing me down. I felt as though I was in some sort of a spin, and unable to pull out. Functioning, yes. But, so far from life as I had known it, or as

I had hoped it would be.

Hope, whatever that was at this point, had moved out of reach, beyond my capacity. But, according to the prophet, not beyond God's. So, I was reduced to waiting . . . waiting . . . waiting for the promised renewal . . . waiting to someday "soar on wings like eagles." What I needed was to see life the way God sees it. But I had no idea how long that would take.

"Oh, God!" I cried out. "Where are You?"

As I prayerfully read through the Scriptures, however, I discovered that God had already asked mankind that very same question. In so doing, He forever placed us squarely before our responsibility to Him . . . and ourselves.

God walked through the Garden of Eden, knowing that His plan had been betrayed by the very ones it had been designed to fulfill. Yet, in spite of it all, God still sought out Adam, the man. On the surface, nothing had changed, yet everything had changed. Though God was still accessible to man, man was no longer accessible to God. "Then the man and his wife heard the sound of the LORD God as he was walking in the garden in the cool of the day, and they hid from the LORD God among the trees of the garden. But the LORD God called to the man, 'Where are you?'" (Genesis 3:8-9).

Shocked into coming to grips with my own life, my own choices, it became clear to me that the question was not so much "Where is God?" but rather "Where am I?" What was it that was standing between us? What expectations did I have that God never intended for me, or for the America I loved? Had certain ideals unconsciously been twisted into the idols that have characterized human history ever since that fall from paradise so long ago? Just where *was* I?

CHAPTER TWO

Why Can't I See Him?

Oh, the depth of the riches of the wisdom and
knowledge of God! How unsearchable his
judgments, and his paths beyond tracing out!
"Who has known the mind of the Lord?
Or who has been his counselor?"
"Who has ever given to God, that God should
repay him?" For from him and through him and to
him are all things. To him be the glory forever!
(Romans 11:33-36)

■

What a Christmas! As I slowly shuffled back to my hut on automatic pilot, deep in thought as I unconsciously placed one foot in front of the other, unanswered questions assailed me to the point where I too was finally left with that shell-shocked 2000-yard stare. It was a look we had all learned to respect—at a distance. Having given a detailed account of the demise of that Cambodian village to "Intell," I felt all talked out. Washed out. I didn't want to see anyone or do anything.

Technically, I was performing well. So what was the problem? Why wasn't it all falling together according to the cool, clipped professionalism that was supposed to transcend the emotions and lead to concrete answers? In the heat of the tropics and the war, my own logic was somehow leaving me cold. This strangely mutated world was rendering my perspective obsolete. Too small. Too confining. Something was missing!

I stepped out of the sweltering heat into yet another Quonset hut that had been scrounged up to provide a little recreation for guys a long, long way from home. In it were the all-important air conditioner, some beat-up furniture, and a fridge. Cold Pepsi and beer! A war zone's lounge. A place where men could get together at the end of the day and talk about what was happening.

But I already knew the larger picture of "what" was happening: superpowers, "containment," war by proxy, "flexible response," treaty commitments—and duty. All of which I still more or less believed, even though in this instance it didn't seem to be working. However, pain was forcing me to go deeper . . . or beyond. Human reasoning just wasn't enough to either explain or justify the suffering I had personally felt, witnessed, and inflicted in my role as a combat pilot. I needed to know "why." Not so much "Why is this happening to America?" or even "Why is this happening to me?"—although that was certainly part of it. Ultimately, I realized that boiling deep inside me was the more universal question, the one God had asked all mankind so long ago: "Why do you do this to yourself? Where are you?"

So where was I?

Geographically speaking, I was in Thailand. And daily I flew over the two Vietnams, Laos, or Cambodia. I was in a war. But where was I really? Psychologically? Emotionally? What did I expect from life? I wondered. Was there still room for God in the midst of all the hopes and dreams I had for myself—and America?

Our world view

From time to time we are all constrained by circumstances to make choices and decide what is crucial to life itself, not only as a person but also as a people. It's the age-old issue of priorities, hard choices. Life is full of them. We're forced to ask, "What really counts?" and, "According to whom?" As soon as we ask those questions—questions for which science, with all its lofty accomplishments, is not equipped to answer for us—we blunder into the essence of philosophy itself, and ultimately religion. We're searching for a system of values for which we will sacrifice in order to get on with life (or at least grimly try to). We are groping for a purpose, the ultimate good . . . a god.

The conclusions we come to are referred to by sociologists as our world view. Or, we could call it the result of our culturally or subculturally imposed norms. These boil down to a vaguely defined mix of inherited attitudes, which determine our values and ultimately dictate our behavior. Attitudes, values, and behavior—it's just that simple. Cause and effect. And though we like to think we're free, the fact remains that based on geography, climate, socioeconomic background, and religion, we have already been profoundly marked by our tribe and our traditions.

Our world view, then, becomes the lens through which we look for purpose and dignity in the events surrounding our lives, whether they are cataclysmic or routine. In conforming to these expectations, we unwittingly adopt a "religion," affirming what we've been taught to affirm and condemning what we've been taught to condemn. In doing so, we hope to find life, meaning, and approval. It's only natural.

But, that's where the problem arises. It's all so natural.

How do we see it?

As I looked into the question of where I was in relation to the unchanging Creator of it all, I was shocked to discover that Paul begins his treatise in Romans by boldly declaring that God is a self-evident fact, clearly revealed in the creation! However, since the Fall, man has been in hiding. That is, he has had his own way of defining life—both seeing it, and not seeing it at all. Paul says, "Although they knew God, they neither glorified him as God nor gave thanks to him, but their thinking became futile and their foolish hearts were darkened. Although they claimed to be wise, they became fools and exchanged the glory of the immortal God for images made to look like mortal man. . . . Therefore God gave them over. . . . They exchanged the truth of God for a lie, and worshiped and served created things rather than the Creator" (Romans 1:21-25).

Probably the most frightening words in Scripture are "God gave them over." Another translation says, "God gave them up." To what? To what they wanted—their world view. The world fails to understand that God does not pressure us to follow His plan—unless we earnestly desire to be pressured! Or to be bridled.

The problem with life is not that we can't have what we want. The problem is that we can! We're free to follow our hopes and dreams, but that also means that we're free to follow our illusions and delusions—and reap their inherent consequences. We're just that free.

If our dreams, however, are no longer submitted to the guiding, restraining influences of God—the One who helps us distinguish between "can" and "should"—to whom will we go for that guidance? Paul continues: "Furthermore, since they did not think it worthwhile to retain the knowledge of God, he gave them over to a depraved mind, to do what ought not to be done" (Romans 1:28).

It's clear that if we think we have a better plan, God will let us follow our own logic. We can live life the way we see it. What we see is what we'll get! Until . . .

Something happens

In his novel *Something Happened*, Joseph Heller describes a middle-class family animated by the American dream.

"Making it" is their focus. But just when things seem to be going right—that is, materially—the central character's relationships start to unravel. The emotional and psychological realities of life can no longer be swept under the carpet of corporate climbing.

As a result, his family becomes a house full of strangers, each with his own life and patterns. Communication is almost nonexistent between husband and wife. As for the kids, it's those teenage years! And at work, the big promotion somehow no longer seems important. Success has had its price and he's not sure it's worth it! A certain listlessness has set in. "What's it all about?"—that crushing mid-life question just won't go away. It all seemed so right, so good, so necessary to fulfillment . . . and so natural! Then, "something happened." And he doesn't know why.

But, neither did I. And it was all the more painful because I loved America so. I had cut my teeth on the idea of the American dream. Filled with hope, my Slavic grandparents immigrated in '04. Ellis Island and the rest. Though they couldn't speak a word of English, their generation passed on to my parents some values that had been fired and hardened in the test of a world depression.

Then my dad's generation literally marched out of that poverty, put ten million men and women in uniform, and moved them to the far corners of the globe with all the machinery necessary to win a world war on two fronts. They were the generation that, though it possessed "the bomb," did not blunder into an empire, but rather rebuilt that tired war-torn world, putting it on a sound financial footing and ushering it into unheralded prosperity. Even great prosperity for its former enemies. This was the generation that had somehow along the way learned to give. And the world at that time was truly needy . . . and was exhausted enough to admit it. An unusual convergence of events.

But the story doesn't stop there. Even after the GI's came home, went back to school on their "bill of rights," and started the "baby boom"—my generation—the momentum created during the war continued to push the nation on in the struggle against totalitarianism. There was the Berlin airlift. Then, Korea. And the world continued to take note that we were not going to retreat . . . or ever again "appease" an aggressor.

From Pearl Harbor to Inchon, a decade forced us to assume superpower status. We were loved by our friends and bitterly hated by our enemies, if for no other reason than for our unparalleled success. It was all so new for us, so different from the isolationist tendencies of the past. We had finally come into our own, confident that we had something to give. Freedom.

But along with that freedom and prosperity came our fears. And McCarthy's inquisition played upon those fears. Communism! The Iron Curtain. The U2. Sputnik. And the Berlin Wall.

With the arrival of a new decade, our young president called upon the generation raised in the habit of victory to "pay any price, bear any burden, meet any hardship, support any friend, oppose any foe, to assure the survival and the success of liberty." Missiles in Cuba seemed to remind us yet again who the enemy of freedom was, and a successful blockade underscored the value of force in dealing with him. So, animated by the idealism that only years of success and affluence can produce, the baby boomers embarked upon the Peace Corps, the Alliance for Progress, the space program, and . . . the boats for Vietnam.

Our history, both personal and corporate, had given us a "truth" for which we were ready to sacrifice. We all assumed in those early days that it would be like it had always been. We were told that the boys would be home by Christmas. And we believed it. Why not? History would certainly repeat itself. Victory. The good guys. But as time moved on, it became apparent that something was wrong.

Something happened! Some new element was being added and it wasn't yet clear. But somewhere, somehow, assumptions had been made—mine, ours, theirs, whoever's—and, in spite of the heroics, a terrible mistake was being enacted before my eyes. Not an American dream, but an American tragedy, far from home. The pain of it all was teaching me the limits of my culture, my world view. Though logical and justifiable, it was incomplete. Truth was proving itself to be much bigger.

World view and truth

Some say that truth is whatever serves the revolution. Others say that the history of a people, their truth, consists of the lies they can agree upon. Still others would say that we cannot hope to know the truth. We can only hope that our "myths" coincide with and, hence, can explain reality enough to give a people a sense of destiny. Sounds rather cynical, doesn't it? But honest historians will tell us just that. They are the first to say how difficult it is to separate myth from reality when digging into the archives.

But no matter how we feel about the truth, it is certain that our cultural lens has colored it, leaving out the painful and embarrassing, and enhancing the acceptable and ennobling. It's only natural. For many, culture alone becomes the final arbiter in determining family, friends, enemies, success, failure, masculinity, and femininity. For the unsuspecting, mere tradition eventually embodies the sum total of life itself. Our way of life. Our "sacred" way of life!

But just how sacred is it? Will our inherited world view, embodied in our traditional approaches, enhance our sensitivity to God and our search for Him? Or will it act like blinders to our eyes, creating expectations that life was never designed by its Author to deliver?

As Paul stood on Mars Hill, surrounded by the success, wealth, and idolatry of Athens, he dared to remind the people that all they had and all they were had been given only as a starting point of their lifelong search for meaning in the God who is so much bigger. The apostle said, "The God who made the world and everything in it is the Lord of heaven and earth. . . . From one man he made every nation of men, that they should inhabit the whole earth; and he determined the times set for them and the exact places where they should live. God did this so that men would seek [or "grope for"] him and perhaps reach out for him and find him, though he is not far from each one of us. For in him we live and move and have our being" (Acts 17:24-28).

Scripture sadly points out that the vast majority of the Athenians rejected Paul's argument, and even found it laughable when he dared to call them to repentance in light of the surpassing glory of God in Christ. They just refused to realize that culture—that unique mix of tribe and tradition—and the world view it creates are only the starting point. It is our launch platform to the sacred, not the sacred itself. It is the means, not the end. In it and through it we are to "grope" for God, exchanging, sometimes painfully, a cultural half-truth for an encompassing personal revelation of God Himself. To refuse this revelation is to eventually blunder into violation of the Third Commandment.

The Third Commandment!

"Thou shalt not take the name of the LORD thy God in vain" (the Third Commandment) is the logical consequence of "having no other gods" before Him (the First Commandment). It has little to do with "cursing" and everything to do with our world view. A culture and people that no longer actively seek God and His plan will eventually try to add His name to any plan the mind can conceive. Vanity!

Taking "God's name in vain" means to use it to justify whatever the individual or corporate body wants to do. Whether it be the subtleties of a civil religion, "my country right or wrong," or the strong temptations of a theology of personal "health, wealth and happiness," we all tend to assume that justice, righteousness, and God Himself are on our side. And it's just not true either personally or corporately. God and His plan encompass so much more! And He will send us messengers to make sure that we don't forget it.

God's messenger

John the Baptist, Jesus, and Paul each went out into the desert, as had Abraham before them, to be alone with God. To do business with Him. Hot, dry, parched, hungry, stressful, and fatiguing business. They were clearly led to do so. And they suffered for it. But, in the midst of it all, they came to grips with their God and His eternal purposes.

But what does "the desert" mean for you and me? It's no different for us than it was for them. Humiliation, suffering, and pain will help us exchange our world view for His. For only when it's painful enough will we finally stand alone before Him and do business with Him. As with Job, when it's painful enough, the words of our well-intentioned mentors and friends will no longer suffice. Like Job, when assaulted by the pious platitudes that seemed so true when things were going well, we will demand that they be proven again in the crucible of our present circumstances. And the fire of the test—the test no one escapes—will burn away the cultural dross of an inadequate world view and teach us once again not so much "what" is essential about life but "who" is essential to life. For that something that is missing . . . is really someone. For all of our culturally defined goodness, we may wind up like Job saying to God, "Surely I spoke of things I did not understand, things too wonderful for me to know. . . . My ears had heard of you but now my eyes have seen you. Therefore I despise myself and repent in dust and ashes" (Job 42:3-5).

I've always found it very interesting that Job, a "blameless and upright man who fears God and shuns evil," had to repent. Of what? It's really not clear. Was it a subtle form of self-righteousness that was unconsciously based on works? An incomplete view of God? These are only human tendencies that we all share. But could it be that there was a particular root cause? Could it be that Job had fallen into the subtle trap of thinking he had it all figured out? That his world view was complete? I can only speculate, but as I studied his life, lying there in my hammock waiting for my next mission, one theme clearly stood out . . .

Pain transformed Job.

And I was coming to see that it would transform me—if I would let it. The heartache of being human was preparing me to listen to and perhaps see the God who would never be reduced to being the servant of anyone's world view. Even an American's! "'My thoughts are not your thoughts, neither are your ways my ways,' declares the LORD. 'As the heavens are higher than the earth, so are my ways higher than your ways and my thoughts than your thoughts'" (Isaiah 55:8-9).

To see God as Job did, I, too, would have to repent of the obviously inadequate world view to which I was so desperately clinging. But, as with Job and everyone else, I resisted because it seemed to be all I had! It made me feel so self-sufficient and capable. Even righteous! But my idealistic, tradition-bound world view was being stripped away. It was like being upside-down, in a spin, out of control.

CHAPTER THREE

Learning to See

We rejoice in the hope of the glory of God. Not only so but we also rejoice in our sufferings. . . .
(Romans 5:2-3)

■

Who really wants suffering? There aren't many people who do. According to Paul, however, not only are Christians to expect suffering; we are to submit to it joyfully. We should "rejoice in our sufferings" (Romans 5:3).

I never really understood why this is true until I gained some insight into the learning process itself while I was in graduate school following the war. With a little time and distance and some research, I began to piece together what I had been through. But now as I look back on all those years, the event that best describes what we must all go through from time to time occurred during pilot training.

The year was '69. We had just put a man on the moon. My flight training class had just completed the basic program in single-engine propeller-driven Cessnas. We affectionately referred to them as the "bug-smashers." However, the next phase would be jets! Our classroom preparation had been intense. We were ready for 'em! Or at least we thought so. The anticipation was mounting.

Finally, that long-awaited day arrived—our introductory flight, complete with helmets, oxygen masks, and parachutes, the paraphernalia of the brotherhood of pilots. Taxi, takeoff, and climb-out had been a piece of cake. However, later, as the instructor pilot pulled the nose of the jet trainer upward and throttled back the power to "bleed off" the airspeed, he began to review yet one more time the maneuver that we were about to perform: a spin recovery! But strangely, I found myself listening to his re-explanation of the maneuver with all the aplomb of the Cheshire cat in Alice in Wonderland.

You see, as an Air Force lieutenant and the young aspirant to a much coveted set of wings, I subscribed to the philosophy that man was captain of his own fate. My world view convinced me that there was nothing a determined individual couldn't do. "Invictus." Like all young men—I already knew! Or, at least I thought I did. You didn't need to tell me. Anyway, you probably couldn't. And I'm sure I conveyed that to those who tried.

You could even see it in the way I walked. Like so many others before me, I strutted out to the airplane that day like a "real pilot." For a generic pilot merely straps himself to the plane, but a *real* pilot straps the plane to himself! Or so I thought, until . . .

The airplane began to shudder. With the engine noise reduced to a whisper and the altimeter "winding up," the airspeed continued to decrease until we were below safe flying speed. As the vibrations increased in intensity, so did my anxiety. Then, as the terminology goes, we "stalled." Though we were several miles up in the air, we were no longer flying! Much in the same way that an autumn leaf falls to the ground, we began to spin out of control.

That moment the left wing literally fell out of the sky and dragged the rest of the airplane along with it. The chaotic sensation suddenly and radically altered my view of how well I was doing in the program. Not even on the wildest of carnival rides had I ever experienced such emotional havoc. Finally being introduced to such strangers as transverse, negative, and positive G-forces left me feeling totally at the mercy of the unknown! With the horizon spinning around me at an ever increasing rate, a few seconds seemed to stretch into a lifetime of experience. As the spin "wound up" and the altimeter "wound down," I grimly realized that the airplane was not strapped to me—I was strapped to it!

But the ride had only begun! My instructor, a senior major with thousands of hours of flying time, routinely entered the spin recovery procedure. He kicked in opposite rudder, which immediately stopped the spinning but slammed my helmet against the canopy. After that, he "bumped" the nose by pushing the stick abruptly forward to break the stall. Now slightly inverted and literally hanging by my seatbelt, he began to pull back on the stick to pull out of the ensuing dive. In the process, he glued me to my ejection seat as the normal force of gravity was multiplied by four or five times.

As my blood began to pool at my feet, "tunnel vision," a sign of lack of oxygen to the brain and the pilot's sure warning of impending blackout, set in. Flexing my leg and stomach muscles, I struggled to maintain consciousness as the pull-out continued.

Then, as if I hadn't had enough, at the apex of the recovery, the instructor added power and eased the nose over, causing the sensation of weightlessness much like the astronauts experience. Within a matter of seconds, I passed from four times my body weight to zero gravity. "There," he said matter-of-factly. "A piece of cake." The plane was now back under control . . . but my body wasn't.

Having left any sense of equilibrium floating somewhere behind us in the Texas sky, the ordeal finally caught up to me! It was all I could do to get my oxygen mask off in time as the pancakes I had eaten for breakfast, also in an apparent state of weightlessness, came *up*! The major had already anticipated such a reaction, for he calmly handed me the all-purpose sack he was accustomed to carrying for "real pilots."

Sticking my head in the bag, I began to . . . "pray": "O Lord! . . . O Jesus! . . . " It must have sounded like I had just found religion! Later, in a cold sweat and still dry heaving, I was in no shape to fly the plane. And yet, somehow, through the fog that now seemed to engulf the cockpit, I managed to appreciate that crusty old professional sitting next to me, even though he was clearly unsympathetic to my plight. The ice man! Having seen it all before, he ignored me and pressed on with the mission by commanding, "O.K.! Now it's your turn to do it! Take us up, put it into a spin, and recover!"

"You've got to be kidding!" I said, bordering on disrespect. After all, who in his right mind would choose to do that again? Now that I knew what it was, I wouldn't have even considered doing it the first time! Everything in me wanted to flee the situation and its inherent humiliation. I had already lost my breakfast. I now seriously wondered whether or not I would be able to control my bowels! Pilots have a lot of cute sayings about such things, and up until that moment I thought they had been kidding! But, there I was . . . strapped to the plane. Trapped. Nowhere else to go but into the next spin.

As I looked again to my instructor for further explanation and, perhaps unconsciously, consolation, all I saw smiling back at me was the Cheshire cat, smug in his knowing aplomb.

The learning process had begun!

The learning process

Looking back on that humiliating scene, I sigh that whimsical chuckle of experience and laugh at myself. What incredible naiveté! How often in my young adulthood had I entered into a situation thinking that I would just "strap" it to me and get on with it? More than I could count. Confidence too often proved to be only that fleeting feeling of control that I had before I'd gathered all the facts! A mere combination of ignorance and, perhaps, arrogant cover-up. Ill-prepared and not knowing it, what I *thought* I knew—my world view—kept me from learning what I really needed to know.

Later, as a pilot who was deemed fully capable of assuming the responsibility of a mission involving the lives of many men and multimillion-dollar machines, I knew intimately and well what had been impossible for me to know up until then: the price of transforming my world view. It takes time to learn what we initially resist, until it becomes the ingrained knowledge of expertise. It requires suffering, an unwanted mix of pain, humiliation, and that desperate effort that comes only from having "been in a spin," so to speak.

Eventually, with time, flying became easy in the sense that I no longer had to consciously think about it. The stick, rudder, and the rapid interpretation of the myriad of instruments were all habits. I simply "thought" where I wanted the airplane to be and in what altitude with respect to the horizon, and my hands and feet did the rest automatically. A conditioned, trained response. Quiet competence. But it all began by overcoming that initial stumbling block to all true learning . . .

Unconscious arrogance

I now know that my conscious efforts and sweat would never have been applied to learning how to fly at all had it not been for that spin. All of life is that way. It has to be. Because of our fallen nature, we tend to have an unconscious arrogance. We explain life from a myopic perspective, with a world view that blocks the learning process, particularly with respect to God and His design for life. We all think we know better! So, from time to time, God, the instructor pilot, allows us to be shocked into conscious awareness of our need.

Just what does it take to get adult men and women, with all their sophisticated self-defense mechanisms in full array, to admit that they are incomplete and in need of new insight and new role modeling? What does it take to begin the transformation process that Paul talks about? A honeymoon soured by the light of day? A mother's hope-filled lullaby of the past, now sung in tears as she watches her child's self-destructive behavior? Or perhaps it might be the highly competitive climb up that corporate ladder (in my case, the one at the Pentagon) only to find the view at the top to be more of the same, or worse—not worth it! In vain. What does it take to make someone want to "turn it around" in order to pick up whatever it is he has missed along the way? Probably a shock of some kind. A spin!

As I recovered from that spin, it dawned on me how easy it had been to unconsciously live out an illusion and how costly it was to exchange that "image" for truth. With my stomach now calmed enough that I could dare to pull my head out of the sack, I began to take inventory of where I was and what would be required of me. Not only was I still in the airplane, but now, stripped of all self-deception, I was face-to-face with the real me, with all of my ignorance.

Though in my pre-spin pride I had been willing to admit that I had "a few things to learn," I just didn't know how many that few would turn out to be! The question was, what would I do now? Could I learn? Would I learn? As I now faced another spin, I was asking myself just that: "How much do I really want this? How much do I want to fly?"

But life, as it often does, had left me no choice. We were only twenty minutes into an hour-long mission. Ejection, at least at this point, was out of the question. So, slowly I moved my hands back to the controls and began to sort out my thoughts. As the instructor waited, I recalled, dimly, what had just transpired, and in newfound humility began to ask a few questions for . . . clarification. No, not really. I was buying time. Though I wasn't quite ready to face the next spin, I had learned quite a bit from the first one. It was now obvious to both of us who the instructor was and just how much the student had to learn. In my own mind, I left my unconscious arrogance behind and became aware of my desperate need to learn.

Conscious acquisition

Strictly business, my instructor answered my questions, which were growing ever more sincere as the inevitable next spin approached. "Three revolutions . . . opposite rudder . . . bump the nose . . . four "G" pullout and level-off." I was consciously acquiring the needed information. Consciously, that is, with all the frontal-lobe mental faculties I could muster, I began to rehearse in my mind what would be needed in the coming sequence of events. I now knew that flying was not going to be like I "knew" it was going to be, and it was not going to conform to my convenience. So if anyone was going to change, it had to be me!

I can still remember my instructor quizzing me, making sure that I was ready as I pulled the nose up. In spite of the fatigue, I was mad enough to "get on with it." I not only needed to show *him*; I needed to show *me*. I had to overcome my fears and doubts. Only conscious mental effort and the discipline that followed would do that. I knew that I needed to overcome myself, my fear-imposed limits. Momentarily, I would be passing into the next phase of the process to prove, I hoped, that I had assimilated the information. And something more . . .

Conscious application

That I hadn't quit! Shocked, yes. Perplexed, yes. Worried, probably so. But, I was still in the air. And as the altimeter wound up and the airspeed wound down—again!—I fleetingly wondered whether or not the instructor had brought another all-purpose bag. My last sign of doubt. Now fully concentrating on the shuddering airplane and its instruments, I didn't have time to ask.

As the right wing stalled and pulled up into a spin, I found that this time the ride was completely different. It was all up to me! I was responsible for the recovery. The instructor had assured me that short of killing us, I would be in control. With my adrenalin pumping, my heart pounding, and my mind clearly fixed on the recovery technique, I consciously applied what the flight manual and the major had said was the proper way to handle the situation . . . and ignored my sensory inputs. I was maturing as a pilot.

The horizon stopped spinning as I kicked in the necessary rudder. After the plane stabilized in a dive, I broke the stall as I had seen it done and began the high-G pullout. Maintaining consciousness—because I had to—I brought the airplane gradually out of the dive, and I eased it over into straight and level flight. It worked. I had consciously applied what the situation called for. I could read the approval in the major's eyes. At that point we both knew I would make it, and he was more than willing to talk me through the reentry and landing procedures as I flew it home.

Taxiing to a stop on the ramp that day, I climbed out of the cramped cockpit a changed man. The parachute that I had strutted out to the plane with earlier now seemed to weigh a little more. I felt tired—very tired. And we had only been up one hour! With helmet and mask in the left hand and, oh yes, burp bag in the right, I discussed the flight with the instructor all the way back to the squadron area. Later, after stowing the gear, I prepared for a thorough debriefing. As everything was discussed in detail and as we pre-briefed the next mission, I noted that the relationship had changed between us. He was still the boss, but I was no longer afraid. I no longer needed to "cover up." I realized that he had my best interests at heart.

Several months later, this same instructor announced a little ahead of schedule that I was ready for my "check ride." For the pilot, the "check" is a controlled opportunity to demonstrate what he has learned. The mission is just to fly the plane: planning how to use altitude and sector boundaries to accomplish basic maneuvers, simulating emergencies randomly chosen by the instructor, and making all necessary radio calls to smoothly enter into the normal flow of air traffic. Conscious application of acquired knowledge. But to simply fly the airplane is not the purpose of Air Force pilot training. The ultimate purpose is to marry the man and the aircraft to a mission.

Little did I realize that passing that check would, in a couple years' time, lead to a stuffy little briefing room in a Quonset hut tucked away in the Thai jungle. With my armed reconnaissance aircraft being readied just a few meters away, I was being asked to live out the final phase and goal of learning.

Unconscious application
Freedom and creativity come when you have internalized the necessary knowledge in any area of discipline to the point where it is second nature. In flying, with the basics mastered, conscious effort is freed up to be applied to a mission. Actual

combat is not the time to be concerned with learning how to fly. There are too many other considerations at that point.

That day when I entered the briefing room, I knew the briefing officer would speak of the weather, reported troop movements, antiaircraft fire, potential targets, timetables, rendezvous points, and the rest. None of these things would have anything to do with actually flying the airplane, yet they would have everything to do with the success of the mission. Training, with all the imposed humiliation and discipline, had freed me to adapt to the realities of combat. Of life.

And so it is with God. We learn to see Him. We do not *demand* to see Him. There are no shortcuts. This is the learning process: confrontation of our unconscious arrogance (our world view), the humility of conscious acquisition of the knowledge of God, the struggle to consciously apply this knowledge to our situation, and then and only then is there the freedom and creativity that come from having made this knowledge an unconscious part of the larger world view. Jesus said, "You will know the truth, and the truth will set you free" (John 8:32).

I now understand just how much was riding on that spin. That was the instructor's message to me. But the second one was my message to him. Perseverance. Openness. Willingness. It all depended upon that initial response. And so it is also with seeing God. Will we allow God to shock us in order to set us free? Free to learn, free to recapture that something special in life that, in spite of successes great and small, we've missed along the way? There is no other way to put Paul's triumphant cry about rejoicing in suffering into perspective. God confronts our world view not to condemn, but, like an instructor who put a plane into a spin a long time ago, to liberate.

Paul finishes his thought about hope and suffering by saying, "but we also rejoice in our sufferings, because we know that suffering produces perseverance; perseverance, character; and character, hope. And hope does not disappoint us, because God has poured out his love into our hearts by the Holy Spirit, whom he has given us" (Romans 5:3-5). Like Job, we may feel that the reason for our suffering isn't clear or justified. God is silent. But Paul reassures us that if we just hang on—persevere—we will not be disappointed. This, the essence of faith, became more clear to me one fateful Easter Sunday when I needed all the ingrained expertise a pilot can muster.

CHAPTER FOUR

The Eyes of Faith!

Against all hope, Abraham in hope believed. . . .
He did not waver through unbelief regarding the
promise of God, but was strengthened in his faith
and gave glory to God, being fully persuaded that
God had power to do what he had promised.
(Romans 4:18-21)

∎

"Room 'ten-shun!"

We all rose to our feet as the colonel entered. Clothed in sweat-stained flight suits, the squadron, ranging in age from those who had chased Mig aircraft over Korea to those who more recently just finished chasing girls on the campus, stood motionless as a profound hush fell across the briefing room. Some loose parts of the inadequate air conditioner made the only noise that dared interrupt the silence that so aptly heightened the gravity of the situation that faced us.

Rumor had it that the colonel had been called to Saigon in the middle of the night to be briefed. And though rumors were often untrue, experience had taught me that the present situation portended something big.

We had been experiencing heavy losses. Fourteen pilots had gone down within just a matter of hours. Their status for the most part was still uncertain, and rescue operations were

51

being readied for a "maximum effort." Everyone, in spite of the news, continued to do what he had been trained to do. But, as professional as we were, it was still very obvious that we needed a word from the top—the big picture. Leadership.

"Gentlemen," the colonel said, striding toward the podium, "please be seated." There he was. The old man. The reassurance that his presence gave us was backed up by his well-proven expertise. We all knew he'd squelch the rumors and "tell it like it is." And as tough as that might be, we were sure that he would clarify our role in the coming events. Lean, confident, and clearly in control, he called his intelligence officer to the podium to bring us up to date.

"Gentlemen," the major said calmly, "all hell has broken loose."

It was Easter of 1972. What we were up against, the military historians now call the Easter Offensive. Consistent with the theme of resurrection, one quarter of a million communist troops emerged from their sophisticated network of underground tunnels and caves after years of preparation to launch a three-pronged attack upon the Saigon government . . . and the American resolve. The Allied forces had not seen the like since the infamous Tet Offensive of '68. Not only had well-equipped soldiers appeared out of nowhere, but with them were tanks and artillery of all sizes, including the full range of antiaircraft guns and missiles.

For several minutes the major moved multicolored position markers up and down the well-sized charts, painting a bleak fresco of friendly troops and refugees retreating in disarray. As the unit numbers of armies and divisions of friend and foe alike rolled off his tongue with computerlike precision, his monotone dirge droned on, leaving no doubt in anyone's mind that the situation was desperate. A massive commitment of airpower would be needed to "buy some time" for the Allies. Having skillfully avoided sowing seeds of panic, the major was nevertheless brutally honest.

He concluded, "You will be up against Migs [Soviet-built jet fighters], SAM's [surface-to-air missiles], and radar-assisted "triple A" [antiaircraft artillery] of all sizes. Are there any questions?"

The silence was deafening.

Consciously or unconsciously, we were waiting for the direction and, ultimately, the needed motivation to face up to it all. Though years of training had prepared us for this moment, eyes glazed over as each pilot was momentarily lost in his own thoughts. Home! Would he ever see it again? Would he have time to write . . . just once more?

As the "old man" regained the platform, he quietly drew a line on the map with the precision that comes from agonizing hours gathering the facts and coordinating the appropriate response with other squadrons. It had instantaneous meaning for us due to the obvious terrain features. The river would be a natural barrier that would slow the enemy advance. As he pointed to it, he slowly turned toward the audience to whom he was senior in both rank and age, and in a near whisper announced, "We'll stop them—here."

And we did.

Faith!

To this day I still ask myself how. What motivated us to take such risks? Why would we do it? I could possibly speak again of professionalism or training. Or, I could discuss the camaraderie that reigned in the squadron and our commitment to one another. We all knew that the next few days would be costly. But we also knew that no effort would be spared in the rescue attempt if one of us went down. However, as foundational as these attitudes were in our decision-making process, there was an even more profound motivation—the motivation that moves the entire world. Faith!

Yes, faith. Though it was not "the faith" spoken of by Paul when he outlined a specific set of beliefs, it was, however, the essence of faith itself. It all boiled down to trust. Reliance. In our case, it meant commitment to the point of risking our lives! Not naively, but based on a quiet confidence that comes from having been prepared and having proven the faithfulness of leadership in past situations.

From that posture, therefore, we could weigh the present based not on the sorrow of the moment or our angry reactions to it, but our expectations of the future. A hope. Ours was that of rescuing our downed comrades . . . if we could just get to them first. However, there was still the reality of an advancing enemy and his relentless search for pilots, the new pawns on the international chessboard of power politics. That day, the man who symbolized our hope said it all in a few words: "We'll stop them—here."

Behind his word was the entire chain of command and the power it could bring to bear upon the situation. But also there was the proven character of a man who had already demonstrated his personal ability and the concern he had for all of us as people, not numbers. So, as each pilot plumbed the depths of his own soul to answer the question, "Why should I do it?" he came to the inescapable conclusion that it was because the old man had said so. The issue then was simply, yet profoundly, who the colonel was and what he had said. Our commitment was dependent entirely on whether or not we thought his word was trustworthy.

We all live "by faith."
Leaving the briefing that day, I was impressed by the audacity of the plan laid before us. When the colonel had finished his summary and asked for questions, there were none because it was all so clear. Having anticipated all our questions, his presentation was brilliant. A textbook case.

However, as I walked back to my Quonset hut to wait for my takeoff time, I, like the others, began to reflect on the "why" of it all. Why should I take these chances? What was my motivation? Sure, I had confidence in the old man. But I kept wondering if that wasn't just a shadow of a deeper meaning and motivation. And though the uniqueness of this situation probably focused the issue more dramatically for me, I became convinced that what I was facing was unique only in degree and intensity, not in kind. We *all* live by faith.

Whether or not we're ready for it, life forces faith on us. Due to reasoning processes based largely on our world view, all of us, at one time or another, make major commitments of time, energy, and emotion before we can know what the outcome of our choices will be. And try as we may to cover our bets, in the final analysis we can't. We all have to lean on the future based on certain expectations. This is faith

By "faith," I had already committed to an Air Force Academy program before I knew whether or not it would be worth it—that is, whether or not it would help me lead a more fulfilled life than I would in any other career. I couldn't be sure, particularly with a war looming on the horizon. Nevertheless, I committed. As a result, the world called me a cadet. I was identified by my commitments—my "faith." Later, "by faith," I committed to a pilot training program, animated by a boyhood dream. I eventually became known by that commitment as well—a pilot.

This principle touches us all. Whether you are a mother daring to bring new life into this world, a businessman simply trying to earn a living, or a student choosing what course to follow, your hopes presume upon the future and call for a commitment in the present. We all live committed lives, even if it's only one of loneliness in an ego trip. Since all commitment is, in the final analysis, "blind," we all live by faith. And to that extent, we are all "religious."

Faith is a verb!

So, how can we be sure? How can we know if it will be worth it? Was I being a fool to put my confidence in the old man? I couldn't know right away. I had to take a risk. Faith, by its very nature, is risk-taking. It's a verb, an action. The squadron simply could not know what tomorrow would bring. No one ever can. Faced with the time-honored dilemma of war, risking life to ultimately save life, would today's risks and losses be justified by tomorrow's peace and prosperity? Two world wars and a "policy action" in Korea had led us to believe so. But, in the midst of my struggle, I felt constrained by the limits of my human nature. Though I was not alone, I knew that this decision to see it through could not be made for me.

As I crawled up into my hammock to await my mission, the engines of those going before me were starting up just a couple hundred yards away. I listened and entered into their routine in my thoughts: preflight check, start engines, taxi instructions, and takeoff. As they rolled onto the runway awaiting their clearance from the tower, I began to pray. I knew some of them would not be coming back. They would risk it all on the word of the old man. And in my heart I already knew that I would, too.

The writer of Hebrews gives us some basic understanding of the nature of biblical faith. "Now faith is being sure of what we hope for and certain of what we do not see. . . . Without faith it is impossible to please God, because anyone who comes to him must believe that he exists and that he rewards those who earnestly seek him" (Hebrews 11:1,6).

What distinguishes biblical faith from other faith? The pivotal statement here is, "He exists." That is, the eyes of faith look expectantly for God, even if the evidence from a human perspective is lacking. Secondly, biblical faith operates on the basis of rewards. That is, God has promised to all mankind that He wants to keep His rendezvous with us in this life. But are we looking for it? Is God part of our world view? If so, just how much?

This covenant between God and man must often be kept in spite of a person's circumstances—rarely, if ever, *because* of them. Though the love of God is clearly unconditional—that is, He accepts us just as we are—it is just as clear that the promise offered by a relationship with God is dependent on our response to Him. That big word "if."

Much of the Old Testament was written in the form typical of an ancient covenant between a benevolent king and his people. A divine contract. "If you will follow or obey me, then I can bless you." The contract gives us reasons for saying yes or no to the images and values that surround us—competing world views. Because of the promises of God, there is an alternative. We have a choice. But as we commit ourselves by moving toward what God has said, others may not understand. It looks too risky.

A biblically based faith, then, like the faith that was being demonstrated by my squadron, is ultimately founded on who the leader is and what he has said. The faith of a believer takes God at His word and chooses accordingly. Though it appears simple to make this distinction, I was discovering that the implications of a more complete trust in God are far from that.

God said to Abraham, "Leave your country, your people and your father's household and go to the land I will show you. I will make you into a great nation and I will bless you; I will make your name great, and you will be a blessing" (Genesis 12:1-2). For the apostle Paul, Abraham's response to God's promise is the key to saving faith. "Abraham believed God, and it was credited to him as righteousness" (Romans 4:3). However, for Abraham to leave Ur, the land of his fathers, a trade center that had amassed great wealth and sophistication, was not the most obvious thing to do. It meant breaking lifelong family ties and radically altering thought patterns and value systems—taking on a new world view. Without the follow-through, Abraham, despite all his desire, would fall back into the same old patterns.

The promise was linked to leaving. The known and familiar had to be abandoned in order to search out a new land and, hence, a new way of life. So he took all that he had and went into the wilderness to build a new nation. "By faith Abraham, when called to go to a place he would later receive as his inheritance, obeyed and went, even though he did not know where he was going" (Hebrews 11:8).

God had been very vocal, revealing His plans to Abraham with enough detail to clearly indicate what his response should be. But there's also another side to faith: the silent years. God had spoken; of that we can be sure. But after that initial promise, God had also been silent. Very silent. Years passed without a sign of the promise being fulfilled, and life was characterized by the desert . . . nomadic wandering . . . and wondering.

Where was God? Where was the promised Heir . . . and heirs? What was God doing? He had spoken so clearly. Why was He now so silent? He had promised "I will bless you . . . and all the peoples on earth will be blessed through you." The promise was one of blessing. Fulfillment. Reward! God had said that He was for Abraham and those who, in the generations to come, would run the risk of believing—acting on what God had said. Faith!

But sometimes Abraham was fearful or felt alone, yet "against all hope, Abraham in hope believed" (Romans 4:18). Having left it all behind and without so much as the promised son in recompense, Abraham wondered about his reward. To this point being obedient had meant being considered a fool, even by his own servants. There had been no visible results. No proof. Just raw obedience. All those years Abraham's trust was in the Person behind the plan, the character and power of the One who had promised. Finally, God spoke: "Do not be afraid, Abram. I am your shield and your very great reward" (Genesis 15:1).

The humiliation, pain, and suffering were necessary to bring Abraham to the point where he could hear just that statement. In God he had it all. The meaning and dignity of our brief existence are found in *Him*, not in what He can provide. God Himself is the greatest treasure . . . and He doesn't come cheaply.

The sophistication of Abraham's own great civilization, with the temple to the moon goddess rising seven stories above that ancient landscape, had to be exchanged if he were to more fully know the God who made it all. That exchange took place in the desert, that special place of humiliation God reserves for those He loves enough to reveal Himself. It is there, stripped of our past and our preoccupations with the future, that we learn what we don't need, and encounter Him who is the answer to our deepest needs. "This is why 'it was credited to him as righteousness'" (Romans 4:22). He believed in the promise and the power of God in spite of the evidence to the contrary. The eyes of faith!

As my mission number approached, I knew that I, too, would have to hope against hope that even though the world seemed to be out of control, it was not. Though I could not see God, I knew that God could see me. And with that knowledge, I had begun to see. God was at work in my life and in the life of my people and the country I loved. I gave Him the right to be silent.

Like the others, I would risk it all on the word of the old man. Outwardly, I would go through the motions. My life in many ways would appear to be no different from any other pilot facing the unknown. But inwardly, my focus was changing. I was no longer naively believing that God owed my country or myself a victory or glory. I was becoming more aware that God did not intend to take sides. There was something much greater at stake. I sensed that God was taking up His own cause in the midst of all the chaos and confusion, leading me into the desert and into direct confrontation with Him and His eternal agenda. I had begun an inner journey of renewal and deepening. As Paul said, "Therefore, we do not lose heart. Though outwardly we are wasting away, yet inwardly we are being renewed day by day. . . . So we fix our eyes not on what is seen, but on what is unseen. For what is seen is temporary, but what is unseen is eternal" (2 Corinthians 4:16-18).

So, as death tugged at my sleeve, I climbed up into the cockpit yet one more time. Signaling the ground crew, I started engines and verified that all systems were thumbs up, ready to go. As I taxied into position to await my takeoff clearance from the tower, I listened to the chatter on the emergency frequency known as "Guard." Pilots were dispassionately speaking of SAM launches, issuing warnings of potential "flak traps," and exchanging information concerning yet another plane that went down. I realized that from this point on, there would be no more time for reflection. The decision had been made. I'd now be operating on instinct. The age-old instinct to survive.

"Nail. . . . You're cleared for takeoff."

Moving the thrust levers forward, the jet props bit into the heavy, humid tropical air, and within moments I was on my way to a rendezvous with desperate men trying to save their downed buddies and the routed Allied forces from annihilation. As the airplane carried me into the sky toward the war, between the vital radio calls a verse came to my mind: "Then Jesus was led by the Spirit into the desert to be tested. . . ." And I prayed.

CHAPTER FIVE
Silent Frequency

I say to God my Rock,
"Why have you forgotten me?
Why must I go about mourning,
oppressed by the enemy?"
My bones suffer mortal agony
as my foes taunt me,
saying to me all day long,
"Where is your God?"
(Psalm 42:9-10)

∎

We all know *about* God—but do we *know* Him? No matter what our profession of faith or lack thereof, life puts it to the test of reality. Is the God we believe in big enough to define it? Is He big enough to help us face life as it comes, with all its joys and sorrows? For life itself is the evangelist. It will sift and test our world view, forcing us to ask that question again and again: "Where are You, God?" I thought I understood that. I thought I had given God the right to teach me.

But, it was Easter Sunday, "O-dark-thirty," and . . .

We had to stop them!

As flood lights illuminated a flight line humming with the normal activity of preparing planes for war—repairs, refueling, and loading ordnance—the pilots walked around their planes, studiously giving the control surfaces, engines, and fuel tanks that final once-over. The preflight check. In the midst of it all, the chaplain could also be seen making his rounds, personally greeting each man just in case anyone wanted to talk—or pray.

My colleagues and I walked past the guarded earth-and-steel revetments in which the planes were parked to protect them from sabotage. Though we had the same basic takeoff times, we would be going to different sectors, where, for the next four hours, it would be our task as "forward air controllers" to report enemy activity and search out targets of opportunity.

Daily we had to make the hard choices of how to control the violence, measuring it out with laser-guided precision based on the strictly defined "rules of engagement" designed to protect the civilian population. Though it was a stressful situation, we had been trained for it and had more or less resigned ourselves to the fact that, for the moment, it was our lot in life. Though as pilots we had been located at different bases in the war zone, our paths crossed often enough in various phases of training, briefing, and fighting that, as much as possible, given the routine turnover of personnel—and losses—we were friends.

We had just eaten our habitual breakfast of pancakes and eggs, and had talked shop. There was a "flak trap" at "Delta 28" on the North Vietnamese border, which had taken a murderous toll on us and our sister squadrons. With the offensive in full swing, the combination of antiaircraft guns and missiles had increased in intensity. After sharing what we had learned of "jinking" and other maneuvers designed to evade enemy fire, we lapsed into that profound silence—that now too familiar whisper of eternity that belied our apparently confident posturing. We all knew that it was death's aroma.

We exchanged knowing smiles and, with time for just one more cup, we changed the subject. It was one of those rare times when we dared to speak of the intimate and personal. Home! For, like myself, these old men of twenty-five would be rotating next month. Just a few more missions! Some would soon be leaving the military to attend to the great American tradition, the family business. And, of course, the wives and kids were waiting impatiently just a long day's journey away. Others would probably go on to high command positions. But all would probably be successful, of that there could be no doubt. Their minds had been honed with a keen sense of responsibility not only for themselves and their families but also for their community and country.

We wistfully spoke of America and the meaning of commitment. In spite of this tragic scene we'd been forced to witness and experience, we felt we'd learned an important lesson. We had traveled all the way to Southeast Asia to find out that everything needed for happiness was back there. Though we readily admitted the system was far from perfect, particularly with the racial tensions that marked the era, we had all traveled enough to know that no one else was doing any better. Liberty and opportunity was (and still is) America's clear, strong message to a world stagnating in economic and political despair. Freedom! That's what America meant to us—in spite of this war.

Finally, because the mood permitted it, I openly asked some of them if they were "believers." There were some embarrassed guffaws and the trite cover-up that so many gave over there: "If God exists, I'm certainly going to heaven—because I've already done my time in hell." When the laughter died down and they saw that I was serious, a few went on to say that they honestly didn't know if God was there and, if so, what He expected of mankind. Many hadn't gone to church since they were kids and felt that the existential questions could be resolved intellectually or philosophically without the help of "mindless rituals." Their attitudes typified the educated, technological age—confidence in science and self.

I agreed with them to the extent that rituals without reasons must eventually be abandoned. But I also said that they were mistaken if they felt that there was no reasonable basis for true religion. Given just some of the alternatives we had been experiencing firsthand, Christ's life and message of love seemed eminently reasonable! The silence that followed my statement indicated that it had impacted them.

As we finished our coffee, a couple of the men nodded their heads in agreement and sincerely admitted they'd really like to talk about it some more. But someone reluctantly announced it was already time to go. The war just wouldn't wait.

We had to stop them! And eventually, we did. But spread out from Hanoi to Saigon were the dozens of pilots that went down in the process.

Among them were some of the men I had breakfast with that morning.

I immediately left my sector and flew to I-Corps to assume the tactical airborne command of rescue operations, in the hope of finding some of those downed pilots still alive. Profoundly relieved, I heard them one by one as they called in on the hand-held radios all pilots carry in their emergency survival vests. Informing me of the kinds of antiaircraft fire they had encountered and of their routine ejection, most were in relatively good shape.

Having hidden their parachutes, they now needed instructions to successfully evade the advancing enemy and to navigate as much as possible through the underbrush to a potential rendezvous point for their helicopter rescue. They told me they could hear the shouts of the enemy beating the bushes, searching for them. All pilots were equipped with revolvers—just in case. Though they were functioning well, maintaining radio discipline, I could hear the understandable anxiety in their voices as, one by one, they talked me into their position.

"Nail, I see you. I'm three to four miles off your left wing. Turn left ninety degrees and I'll give you a countdown."

"Roger."

"Steady. Now turn right ten degrees. That's it. Ten seconds...5...4...3...2...1. Ready. Ready. You're over me right now. Mark. How copy?"

"Roger. Copy 5-by." I rocked the wings of my aircraft over each position as I climbed out to reassure them that I had made mental note of the terrain features that would later be used to lead the helicopters to them. But first, we had to "neutralize" the area.

In recent years, downed pilots had become invaluable to Hanoi as bargaining chips on the negotiating table at the Paris peace talks. The folks back home were wearing memorial bracelets and the airways were filled with talk of the prisoners. P.O.W. was a national preoccupation—and rightfully so.

But a downed pilot also served as bait in the cold-blooded realities of war. That is, he would be seemingly overlooked by the enemy as heavy antiaircraft guns were moved in and hidden as much as possible around him . . . waiting in deathly silence for the rescue attempt to begin. Unfortunately, this was their fate. As the decision to risk their rescue fell upon me, I came to the sad conclusion that the area was just "too hot."

With their positions being surrounded by mobile antiaircraft guns and with the radar of the missile sites in the north "painting" all the aircraft in the vicinity, our efforts to neutralize the area, to be effective, would require more time. Perhaps several days. I had just reached that decision when I, too, took a hit. Forced to leave them there, I called for another FAC to replace me and the rescue operations continued. As I was leaving, one of them said it for all of them: "Hey, Nail, am I going to have to spend the night down here with Charlie?"

"I'm afraid so."

And they did. For six more days, we flew round-the-clock missions, literally hundreds of them, concentrating the fire power of the Navy and Air Force fighters upon a small area just south of the so-called demilitarized zone in an effort to force the enemy and the jungle to give us back our own. The DMZ of the famous Geneva accords became the most fought-over spot in the world! And though there were global implications, with Paris, Hanoi, Moscow, and Washington vitally interested in the outcome, the reason behind the fighting for the men in the 23rd Tactical Air Support Squadron was personal, not political. A very determined foe was threatening our friends and . . . we had to stop them!

For myself, it seemed that the whole war had boiled down to saving my comrades. We just had to! I was sure we would do it, so sure. Up until now we'd been lucky. Day after day, one or two at a time, we brought them back in a costly slugfest, forcing the enemy to relent under extreme punishment. Many of the men had to navigate by compass to a "safe zone" several miles from where they were forced to punch out. There the helicopters would move in to make the rescue.

With the adrenalin coursing through their veins, my buddies were literally running for their lives. Hiding by day, traveling by night, they were doing all they could to avoid capture, and at the same time moving out from under the antiaircraft guns that stood so ominously between them and freedom. After several days, I and the other pilots assigned to the rescue had learned to recognize their voices and their moods as they kept us informed of their movements—and those of the enemy. Friendships deepened.

I had been orbiting near them or over them for six days trying to prepare their rescue, sharing information, and occasionally cursing with them as the frustration mounted. We'd come so close. So close! But, there was always another gun to kill, a missile site to be silenced, or enemy troops so close that the men couldn't even talk on the radios. So they waited . . . and waited. And so did we. They'd been so brave. "Hang on, man!" I'd say over and over, "We need some more time. Just another day or two. Hang on! With a little more luck. . . ."

And then all was quiet. We had just silenced the missile site and another heavy gun had been destroyed. At last, it looked as though we just might be able to get all of them out, but my aircraft was vibrating, that telltale sign of battle damage. I wouldn't get to cover the helicopter or the actual pickup and egress from the area. After all the time and effort, I would miss the traditional champagne celebration that awaited the rescued and their rescuers when the helicopters safely landed at the base. As the vibrations increased, I turned the rescue over to my replacement and wished the guys on the ground, "Good luck!"

But our luck was running out.

I left my radios on their frequency as I coddled my crippled craft back to "home plate." I overheard the final evaluations and briefings between those on the ground and those in the air. The helicopter was hovering in a safe area waiting for the go-ahead. These men were the most vulnerable of all, the reason why we had to be so sure the area was no longer hot. The men in the chopper had to hover and wait for a period of about a minute for those men on the ground to make that final dash to the chopper and safety. During that time, the men in the helicoper would be a sitting duck for any ground fire. They counted on our evaluation of the situation, for they had little or no armament. When the final clearance was given, it was based on our assessment that it was safe.

Now, fifteen minutes later and not quite back to home plate, I was making an emergency approach to the runway, but at the same time I was riveted to the rescue frequency as I heard the final clearance being given: "Jolly Green, you're cleared for rescue." Seven days of fighting had been reduced to the next minute.

In my mind's eye, I saw the chopper racing in over the treetops to go into a hover. It would only be a few more seconds now. The guys would break from their hiding places like open-field runners going for a touchdown. But, as they approached the helicopter . . .

"We're under fire! We're under fire!" broke in over the radios. "We can't wait . . . we've got to get out . . . we've taken a hit . . . we're taking hits . . . my copilot's hit . . . Oh! God . . . we're going down . . . we're going down!"

Then, the FAC broke in, "The chopper's going down! . . . My God! . . . The chopper's exploded! . . . a ball of flames! . . . a ball of flames! . . . My God . . . my God . . . They've hidden some heavy machine guns . . . It's a trap! . . . The rescue's off . . . Sorry, guys . . . Not today . . . not today."

So far away, yet, united through the radios, my heart went down with that helicopter. I had been so involved for so long that I, too, called out on Guard frequency and was met with silence . . . deathly silence. Nothing . . . nothing! Changing the frequency in desperate hope, I tried yet one more time. And the silence of those voiceless airwaves screamed until I finally realized that all my options were exhausted. We'd lost them. It was over. Over! At that moment, as the war stood still, that same silence whispered to me . . . and spoke of eternity. An entire crew was gone!

I landed my crippled aircraft in tears.

Taxiing in, I knew that when they patched it up, I would be back out there. The slugfest would continue and so would our rescue attempts. Men were counting on us. Little did I realize that this bloodbath would go on for weeks. It became one of the few times in this protracted state of guerrilla war when large armies surfaced in an all-out effort to annihilate one another. And the lives of a handful of men were still hanging in the balance . . . leaving us no choice. We had to do it.

We had to stop them!

Though I was exhausted when I climbed out of the cockpit, my anger was mounting. I didn't understand. We'd come so close. We'd invested so much. Day in, day out, from the briefing to the mission, and back to the briefing room again for the next mission—so it had gone. Around the clock with minimum crew rest. Life had been a whirlwind, and its vortex was the hoped-for rescue. But now, for me, that was gone and only a flurry of activity was left.

And some angry, unsettled questions.

What was "wrong" with trying to rescue a friend? What's "wrong" with that? Why was I so profoundly disappointed? With only enough time to eat and sleep before the next mission, I, nevertheless, reached for my Bible. The question was back. "Why? . . . Where is God?" I thought I had dealt with all this. Why were the questions back? Because the disappointment was so deep and personal. It had all taken a slightly different twist. An angry one. What right does God have to confront us the way He does—and remain so silent?

CHAPTER SIX

A Soldier of Faith

"Even today my complaint is bitter; [God's] hand is heavy in spite of my groaning. If only I knew where to find him; if only I could go to his dwelling! I would state my case before him and fill my mouth with arguments. I would find out what he would answer me, and consider what he would say."
(Job 23:1-5)

■

Enough of this silence! What right does God have to treat us this way? What reasons could He give? In my bitterness and anger I, too, wanted to find out "what He would answer me." Like Job, I demanded some answers. But, also like Job, I could no longer tolerate the mere opinions of men. Too much had transpired for me to put up with the insults of Christian clichés. My anger was too great!

God Himself had to speak! But would He? How? When? I didn't know. But I did know that only He would be big enough—bigger than my rage. I cried out in prayer, lost somewhere between deep faith and angry, cynical despair. But . . .

At the debriefing, it was business as usual.

I walked in, covered with sweat, fatigue, and the after-effects of it all. The room hummed with crews coming, going, and mixing with the Intell staff to exchange vital information. Position markers were being rearranged on the wall-sized charts at the far end of the room. A cloud of smoke hung at eye level, relatively undisturbed by the slow-turning ceiling fan as air conditioners strained to absorb the heat and odors of overworked bodies operating on adrenalin and coffee.

I sat on a large desk in the corner, stared at the floor, and waited. I knew when the crew in front of me finished, I would be asked the routine questions: "Sector? . . . Flying time? . . . Targets discovered? . . . B.D.A.?" [bomb damage assessment]. And finally, "Any unusual activity to report?"

I thought, any unusual activity to report? By that, do they mean a chopper crew that went down? No. Not in war. That's not unusual. There's a category for that. That's to be expected. Routine.

So . . . I tried to think of something else. That new missile site? No, I already reported that—yesterday.

The chopper!

Now, let's see. What about that troop movement near Snoopy's nose on the river? No, that was listed under potential targets.

The *chop*per!

Well, there was what looked like a staging area. No. That would also be under potential targets.

The *chopper*!

Well . . . apparent jamming of the combat frequency?

The chopper! No, the previous crew had already reported it. What about . . .

THE CHOPPER! My God, the chopper went down—a ball of flames—and the odor of failure and death, something air conditioners could never remove, still lingered in the air.

Fighting back the pain and tears, professionalism answered, "No, no unusual activity to report." I left the room realizing that if I had screamed what I really felt, the system could not have handled it. The category didn't exist. Unless you gave it the label of "combat fatigue" or "post-traumatic syndrome." For, as cool and detached as the players tried to be in this game—and in any game!—reality, that is, reality's Author, has His own category, whether we like it or not . . . a divine encounter.

I didn't like it . . . and I didn't want it. But, neither did Job. Nevertheless, God spoke to him out of the "storm" of his own life: "Then the LORD spoke to Job out of the storm: 'Brace yourself like a man; I will question you, and you shall answer me. Would you discredit my justice? Would you condemn me to justify yourself?'" (Job 40:7-8).

Are we so angry about our circumstances that we refuse to listen or even look for God? Do we condemn the God of creation because we don't like our situation? Many people do. Job almost did. But in doing so, he came very close to cutting himself off from the answer. His near condemnation of the God who, for His own eternal purposes, permitted Job's plight, was in a very real sense his own condemnation. Like myself, he was refusing the humiliation of the learning process and the deeper knowledge of God that is promised to us all.

As I reached for my Bible, ready to condemn, to argue, and to justify, I met another soldier . . . a general. Joshua. Joshua was a man who had been trained for battle at Moses' side. He had seen victory and had played a central role in equipping and eventually leading the children of Israel into battle. A man of demonstrated confidence in the promise, he nevertheless felt the loneliness and doubt that any leader experiences. He, too, asked the question, "Where is God?" That is, where does He stand in the affairs of men?

Now when Joshua was near Jericho, he looked up and saw a man standing in front of him with a drawn sword in his hand. Joshua went up to him and asked, "Are you for us or for our enemies?"

"Neither," he replied, "but as commander of the army of the LORD I have now come." Then Joshua fell facedown to the ground in reverence, and asked him, "What message does my Lord have for his servant?" (Joshua 5:13-14)

As the leader who would have to plan the attack, Joshua had been scouting out the terrain near Jericho and was probably circling the imposing fortress city with its renowned walls when he encountered a man "with a drawn sword." God Himself, or His angelic messenger, appeared to Joshua—as a soldier. A Soldier to speak to a soldier. And the Soldier—God—was here to speak to another soldier—me. The message was simple, but profoundly disturbing: God does not take sides. He's on His own side. So the question was turned, yet again, on Joshua . . . and on me: "Who's serving whom?"

For, God is God! He has His design for mankind . . . and for a man. One that He's willing to reveal in us and through us if we will only let Him. The question was: Could I see my struggle in that light—in light of eternity? I asked for greater understanding—and prepared for the next mission. For, the war was still with me. . . . We had to stop them!

"Who are You, Lord?"

Had I not experienced the personal assurance that God was moving me into a larger frame of reference, I would have essentially remained in my self-righteous anger. I would have walked off in a huff and slammed the door on God . . . or at least tried to.

The war was proving to be much more than a disappointment to be forgotten as soon as possible. It was making a categoric statement about the nature of life itself. Was it an absurdity ruled by the passions of men? If that were true, then God was little more than the silent, stony idols decried by the prophets or the Olympian deities the educated Greeks and Romans of Paul's day only paid lip service to. Inventions whereby man could be manipulated—by other men. In many ways, "the opiate of the people." Armed with that philosophic bias, a man would be free to live his life as a "realist," as the gods of his wants and dreams dictated. And logically so.

However, Paul's arguments to the contrary were overwhelming. There was a plan. God had an eternal agenda and was gradually leading men like myself into confrontation with it. Though I didn't like it, and though I honestly questioned whether or not He even had the right to treat me so, as I examined the evidence, I, too, fell on my face before Him and, like Paul, asked "Who are You, Lord?" (Acts 9:5).

The Creator

Paul's opening argument in the book of Romans declares that God is a self-evident fact! "What may be known about God is plain to them, because God has made it plain to them. For since the creation of the world God's invisible qualities— his eternal power and divine nature—have been clearly seen, being understood from what has been made . . ." (Romans 1:19-20).

As gripping a premise as that was to me, unaccompanied by a logical argument it seemed little more than wishful thinking. Too "Pollyanna" to cut it in the world I was facing. With time, however, I became convinced that the creation does impose upon the mind of the mature individual the basic question: "Why?" Why is there something instead of nothing? Where did it all come from? And for what ultimate purpose?

From my own technical background, I realized that

though science was good at explaining the makeup of the universe, the meaning of it all, the why, was essentially a philosophic or religious issue. For a magnificent design logically implies the existence of a designer, a plan. No matter where we look or how we measure it, what has been made is designed to reveal certain aspects of the maker.

God's power, on display in the heavens, declares His omnipotence, that awesome aspect of an immense God beyond our mastery or comprehension. The God to be feared. But He is not a blind force operating by random chance as we have been led to believe in our day and age. For His very nature is revealed not just in the grandeur of galaxies but also in the intricate detail that surrounds us. Whether it be a snowflake or even the microcosm of the atom itself, we see that this incredible Being called God is focused harmoniously on a plan. The power of God is subjugated to a design governed by laws, and that design works itself out, whether in eons or nanoseconds, in artistic, minute detail, leaving the greatest of minds standing in enlightened awe. As Albert Einstein said, "My religion consists of a humble admiration of the illimitable superior spirit who reveals himself in the slight details we are able to perceive with our frail minds. The deeply emotional conviction of the presence of a superior reasoning power, which is revealed in the incomprehensible universe, forms my idea of God."[1]

So, whether we are looking through a telescope or a microscope, God's work is on display. As we meditate upon that fact, we come to realize, as Einstein did, that our critical faculties were not bestowed on us by creation's Author to replace our need for Him but to discover Him through the disciplined use of those faculties. Proven. Revealed. Einstein went on to say, "The cosmic religious experience is the strongest and noblest mainspring of scientific research."[2]

But for those of us of a more humble level of mind and

experience, the colors of yet one more sunset should lead us to exult with the psalmist when he says, "The heavens declare the glory of God . . ." (Psalm 19:1). As a result, Paul declares that in spite of our pretensions to the contrary, ". . . men are without excuse" (Romans 1:20). In our hearts we know that a supernatural intelligence exists. God is there.

But what of man?
It was one thing to admit that God's presence is the moving force behind it all—the primal cause—and quite another to say that He is personally involved or that He cares. We find the psalmist wondering the same thing. "When I consider . . . the moon and the stars, which you have set in place, what is man that you are mindful of him, the son of man that you care for him?" (Psalm 8:3-4).

George Gaylord Simpson, world respected paleontologist who for years was one of the leading spokesmen of evolutionary theory, has taken the psalmist's simple question of our apparent loneliness in the universe, which at times plagues us all, and turned it into a bold assertion: "Man stands alone in the universe, a unique product of a long, unconscious, impersonal material process, with unique understanding and potentialities."[3]

For many in the scientific community, the evidence for an "impersonal material process" seems to be irrefutable, in spite of the growing number of scientists who now clearly feel otherwise. It is in this area of the unique understanding and potentialities of man that the outcome of this debate will be most felt.

We're back to the question, "What is man?" Man initiates, observes, and for some reason feels the right to make a value judgment as to whether or not some activity is a viable cultural expression. For that matter, our whole legal system with its trial by jury is based on the assumption that the judgment coming from reasonably prudent persons is trustworthy. Is all that by "accident," or is man a reflection of something more? Or *someone* more?

The revelation of conscience

If the forces that brought us into being are impersonal, then why are we endowed with all these personal aspects? Why, if we're just another animal, do we rise above instinct to care? To love to the point of self-sacrifice? My contact with Taoists in Asia and in recent years with animists in Africa has taught me that there are some universally shared ideals about what is good and noble in man.

Though the format varies from culture to culture, the basic goodness of a person or his contribution to society can usually be measured in such dynamically equivalent terms as loyalty, faithfulness, honesty, and the very unfashionable concept of self-sacrifice. Though there are scattered tribal exceptions to the basic tendencies—for example, where treachery is touted as virtue—they only serve to highlight the general rule. Man is universally marked with what the apostle Paul calls conscience, that inner voice that speaks of what's best for a man and his tribe: "Indeed, when Gentiles, who do not have the law, do by nature things required by the law . . . they show that the requirements of the law are written on their hearts, their consciences also bearing witness, and their thoughts now accusing, now even defending them" (Romans 2:14-15).

The law written on our hearts whispers to us of social justice and personal integrity—even to the point of self-sacrifice. Consciously or unconsciously, we measure ourselves, our neighbors, and our society through the grid of conscience. Though certainly influenced by our personal maturity and breadth of experience, nevertheless, something in us either affirms a situation, tolerates it, or is outraged by it. Where does that cry for justice come from? The psalmist answers, "Does he who implanted the ear not hear? Does he who formed the eye not see? . . . Who will rise up for me [God] against the wicked? Who will take a stand for me against evildoers?" (Psalm 94:9,16).

Many people feel that the mere existence of evil is a definitive argument against the existence of a loving God. The psalmist implies the contrary. The outrage of our conscience tells us that the self-serving brutality of man is still considered to be wrong. As this kind of behavior makes the evening news, the commentators seem to unconsciously yet unanimously say, "See, this does not conform to the dictates of conscience!"

Therefore, since the evil side of man exists—and only a child would say otherwise—no matter where it exists, even in the most repressive of regimes, we still find those who rise up against it. Risking their own lives for their concept of justice, they are willing to take a stand. Could not their outcry be interpreted as that of the Creator who made us all? What more effective way to reveal His approval or disapproval than to give that message flesh and blood, and a voice? What better way to awaken His image in men than to send a man?

The men of conscience
"Above all, you must understand that no prophecy of Scripture came about by the prophet's own interpretation. For prophecy never had its origin in the will of man, but men spoke from God as they were carried along by the Holy Spirit" (2 Peter 1:20-21). As I studied the scroll that unrolled before me in the pages of Scripture, I saw God choosing man after man, often against their will, to be His message bearer. There were times when the history of God's people seemed to hang suspended between fulfillment and

damnation. At each of these crucial junctures, the plan was rescued from apparent oblivion by some inspired man. Though on occasion a man of God spoke of the future, most often he spoke of the here and now. He dared to cry out for righteousness, justice, and the God-given dignity of all men. The promise! It was the blessing God had entrusted to Abraham so long before, but each generation had to discover it anew.

So, again and again when God had to speak He chose a man to do it. One such man was a prince who, in his own search for meaning, had previously rejected the treasures and pleasures of Egypt. His conscience was inflamed with a mission when he heard God's voice speaking from a burning bush, "I have indeed seen the misery of my people in Egypt. I have heard them crying out because of their slave drivers, and I am concerned . . ." (Exodus 3:7).

Moses reminded the people of the plan. Liberation! The Promised Land! New Life! However, they were reluctant, skeptical, and fearful. Pharaoh's power was not to be trifled with. But with Moses, there was power of another kind. Plagues descended, the sea parted, and the people were delivered. But they didn't really know by whom. They had been in captivity too long. Their world view was so faulty that they still attributed this miraculous deliverance to the idols they brought with them into the desert. So, God spoke through Moses again: "Thou shalt not . . . !"

Moses tried desperately to teach the people of Israel that happiness could not be found outside the moral constraints of true love—the law that is already written on the heart. God wanted to build a nation to be a model of this love, a light to all the nations, the fulfillment of the promise to all men. But for that generation, the desert was death. The fear of the unknown was too great. They did not listen or obey. They refused to believe that they could not take their idols into the Promised Land. They refused to believe that there was something better. So they and their idolatrous influence wasted away in the desert. History was cleansed.

The children had watched all this time as their parents clung so desperately to all that was not essential for life and love. For them, the desert was the necessary purging that led to victory in the Promised Land. Fear had finally given way to faith and to a generation whose conscience had been trained by the law to see the dignity only God could give. Moses had left his mark on history—and on Joshua.

But Joshua, as it is with someone of any new generation, had to encounter the living God for himself. And so a Soldier carrying the flaming sword of God's purpose in history spoke to him. Jericho fell and the people were ushered into the Promised Land.

While the people of Israel listened to the men of conscience, they prospered. But Solomon and his successors forgot, and led the people back into idolatry. Civil war led to calamity and, once again, captivity. In Babylon, the prophets spoke once more, and the promise lived on. A generation was prepared to return to the Promised Land, and they did. The homes, the walls, and the Temple itself were rebuilt. Vineyards and crops were planted and God's blessing was once again experienced. Until . . .

There was Greece. Then, Rome. And the prophets were silent for four hundred years! Then, in occupied Jerusalem, there were whispers and rumors of a Messiah.

The Christ

"In the past God spoke to our forefathers through the prophets at many times and in various ways, but in these last days he has spoken to us by his Son, whom he appointed heir of all things, and through whom he made the universe" (Hebrews 1:1-2). Immanuel! God with us! It was too good to be true. As the incredible story unfolded before my eyes, I saw God Himself living out His eternal agenda in the flesh: working, eating, drinking, teaching, and, when necessary, defying the corrupted traditions of the day so that all would see how revolutionary a new commandment could be: "Love one another."

Oh, how they came to see Him! There were businessmen with financial worries, churchmen who had strayed from the essentials, doctors who had discovered the limits of their cures, governors who knew the limits of their power, and the wealthy who knew the impoverishment of their wealth. And, of course, there were also the sick, blind, leprous, and other outcasts, who came along with the multitudes of the poor.

Each person was very different, yet similar. Each in his own way had been broken by his definitions of life—by his world view. And each discovered that the greatest handicap to overcome was himself. Life had somehow moved beyond the grasp of all these people, exhausting their hoped-for solutions, leaving them faced with their ever-present fears. They all came to Christ needing something more just to get on with life. They felt compelled to know the meaning of life itself, to have a divine encounter.

Another soldier

At this point in my own odyssey, I ran into a fellow officer. He was more mature than I was. He'd already seen many campaigns. He knew the vice of victory and some of the pain of defeat. But through it all, he had been faithful to his training and conscience. He was mature enough to realize that often it is a soldier's lot to face the sad realities of life—the strife of the human condition. Often, as a commander of the occupation forces, he had to face the real decision where to draw the line between the necessary use of force and atrocity. But he had proved himself to be competent and was respected by friend and foe alike.

However, in recent months, life had moved beyond even his ability to understand. In spite of the stoicism in which his Roman world view was shaped, this centurion began to seek another explanation. As he aged, he had seen enough of Caesar to begin to see through him. As for the alternative, the gods, his experience taught him that the borrowed Olympian deities his people worshiped were in reality powerless and better left in the realm of myth, left to those who had no stomach for reality. His training had been too hard and he had seen too much. He was a realist. But now . . .

His friend was sick, dying. Wars, politics, occupation forces, and the rest he understood. But death and separation from a friend was proving to be too much. Eternity was becoming heavier than he could bear. However, he had heard of a man from Galilee. There had been rumors of healings, and even resurrections. Of course, he'd been in Palestine long enough to hear all kinds of rumors of prophets and messiahs. But somehow this one seemed different.

As he followed the wispy trail of hearsay evidence and rumor, he was astounded by the people he ran into along the way. They were sure they had been in the presence of God. They spoke of lame people who could now walk, the blind who could now see, and always they spoke of forgiveness and love. Not only had their situation changed, but so had their outlook.

After the centurion found Him, he waited and watched from afar. He had never heard a man speak like this. But his heart slowly became convinced as he heard the words that lifted the weight of eternity from him. So he approached the Christ in the dignity of his position, but also in newfound humility. He understood the chain of command. He gave orders and expected obedience. Recognizing Christ's authority, he described his plight. His pride now broken, his eyes pleaded for help.

In spite of the fact that this man was the sworn political enemy of His people, Jesus responded. Complimenting his faith, He said, "Go! It will be done just as you believed it would" (Matthew 8:13). Jesus did not demand that he renounce his profession, for He knew that this side of eternity would be marked with "wars and rumors of wars" (Matthew 24:6). Jesus, too, was a realist. Armies would always be a part of the human condition. But He had come for all men—including soldiers.

Though Christ's disciples, still caught up in the politics of their day, clearly did not understand, as I read that passage, facing the struggles unique to a soldier, I did. Faith had given the centurion access to God's grace in spite of the harsh realities of his duties.

For God was not silent in the sense of being indifferent. He was silent in the sense of being subtle. He has been waiting for us much longer than we have been waiting for Him. Through the creation, the conscience, men of conscience, and finally the Christ, God has spoken and is speaking to us still, offering nothing less than Himself. But we, like the centurion long ago, must come to Him.

My struggle now was to live in light of that amazing grace.

NOTES:

1. Lincoln Barnett, *The Universe and Doctor Einstein* (New York: Wm. Morrow and Co., Bantam Books, 1972), page 109.
2. Barnett, *The Universe and Doctor Einstein*, page 109.
3. Duane T. Gish, *Evidence Against Evolution* (Wheaton, Ill.: Tyndale House Publishers, 1973), page 10.

CHAPTER SEVEN

The Freedom Flight

What shall we say, then? Shall we go on sinning so
that grace may increase? By no means!
(Romans 6:1-2)

■

It was about midnight when I landed. Rescue operations had worn us all down, leaving us fatigued, empty, needing something. After debriefing, as I walked to the Quonset hut that masqueraded as a pilot's lounge, I heard the double-tongued saxophone belting out those sensual melodies designed to excite the libidos of lonely men in an audience with a lone woman dancing on a stage.

She was an olive-skinned, dark-eyed beauty with jet black hair. Though only twenty, her face spoke of so many years more. While still a youthful Buddhist believer in the village, her father sold her to someone from Bangkok, where she was brought under the pretext of getting married. At least, that is what she had been told.

But, now on the stage, her innocence having long ago been sold by her mercenary "husband," she took out her sadness and pain in the only avenue open to her: contempt.

Undulating to the beat of the drum, she skillfully manipulated the audience through her eyes, her mouth, and, eventually, her clothing, to achieve her bitter feline ends. Though the men did temporarily forget the war, in her scorn-filled domination of them she became one of the war's most tragic casualties.

Sitting there in the midnight tropics, I caught a glimpse of myself . . . her . . . the others. In the midst of the heat, my blood began to cool. Dancing before me was no longer an object but a person—and a victim. Though I had not chosen any part of this war, as tired as I was, I still had choices to make. Even though her seductive smile was often cast like a net in my direction . . . grace prevailed. While all eyes were fixed on the object of their desire, I rose unnoticed from the bar and silently sought the exit, while the cheers and whistles muffled the door slamming shut . . . on a page in my life. Amazing grace!

By then the war had made it clear to me that man without God lives in a spiritual vacuum. He needs something, but he doesn't know what. Often, to avoid asking the hard questions, he tries to fill this personal void with activities or things. In doing so, he proves in the spiritual realm what is already common knowledge in scientific quarters: nature abhors a vacuum. Where one exists, all sorts of things will rush in to try to fill it.

Though the temptations in Nam were numerous and varied, the source was the same. Far from the routine and stabilizing influences of home, the spiritual vacuum became more and more pervasive. It was not only a question of a war and how we conducted ourselves while we were on duty that marked our lives but also a question of what we did while we were off duty. Though none of us had chosen the particulars of this war, there were still choices to be made. And the pressure was on. We had to stop them!

One day during a routine preflight inspection, I discovered that the center-line fuel tank had not been filled. Normally I'm not one to lose my temper. But this time I was livid. In going out to fly a rescue mission, I could have easily become the one that needed rescuing. I shouted at the young sergeant who had been responsible for the aircraft's maintenance. "How could such an obvious thing have been overlooked?!"

At first I thought his silence stemmed from the shocking realization of how grave his error had been—a matter of life and death. But as I removed the very dark glasses he was sporting, I was stunned to realize that "no one was home." Drugs! That 2000-yard stare that comes not from combat but from chemicals. Due to our proximity to the golden triangle, heroin and its derivatives were too easily procured, particularly by the youngest among us. It was a two dollar trip out of hell, the price of a fix. So tempting. Choices! For many men the vacuum was filled with careless if not callous indifference to the consequences.

I had a rendezvous time to keep, so I ordered him to his quarters and took the standby aircraft. When I returned, he was there to meet me. My temper had cooled, so we began to dispassionately discuss what he was facing: a less than honorable discharge that would follow him the rest of his life.

He was silent, trying desperately to digest the truth about himself. So, I stepped out of role and asked a few penetrating questions in an effort to find out why. The confusion that filled his explanation left me with no doubts. He was lost. In his own way, he was a victim. At nineteen, he was just too young to be loading bombs in a war no one seemed to understand. Reaching into my flight suit, I pulled out the pocket New Testament I was in the habit of carrying and gave it to him—along with a second chance.

A few weeks later, he was performing well and seemed

to be rather motivated for life. He showed me to my airplane and waited rather awkwardly as I gave it the once-over. I sincerely complimented his work, and then I asked what his plans were for the future. He spoke of going to school on the GI Bill, and perhaps making up with a girl back home that he hadn't "treated so good." Then he pulled the New Testament out of his pocket and thanked me.

"Don't thank me," I said. "Thank God!"

Amazing grace!

"Since we have been justified through faith, we have peace with God through our Lord Jesus Christ, through whom we have gained access by faith into this grace in which we now stand" (Romans 5:1-2). Faith ushers us into God's perspective on life, opening our minds to new vistas of promise. But it is God's grace that empowers us to live there. When we catch a glimpse of ourselves as we really are, painful as that may be, our need for spiritual growth becomes clear. The vacuum will be filled! We will make choices—or fail to. At the point of decision, faced with the grey areas that touch our own souls and the souls of others, we either consciously or unconsciously begin to look for grace. We sense the need for the knowledge and the means to master not so much a presumed hostile world that surrounds us, but rather our greatest enemy: ourselves. It's a matter of choices.

Two kinds of pilots

It's been said that there are two kinds of pilots: those who have landed with the landing gear still up, and those who are about to. As absurd as that sounds, there is some truth to it, as one of my colleagues found out. Coming down the glide slope just a few yards off the runway, he pulled back on the stick to round out and touch down only to be met by a sinking feeling in the pit of his stomach.

However, that sinking feeling was not his imagination. With his landing gear still in the wells, he sank right into the runway. Fortunately, his empty wing fuel tanks absorbed the shock intended for his landing gear. Skating along the runway at over a hundred miles an hour produced an unforgettable display of sparks for all who were there to see— including the colonel. It was only a small miracle that kept the residual fumes in the tanks from exploding.

Up until that point, this young pilot's problem drinking had been quietly tolerated. The "old man" had ordered the bartender to limit, as gracefully as possible, his consumption. But there was always the flash of his flask, representing a certain amount of John Wayne-style independence—and a pitiful dependence. As it is with any group of professionals, there was some social drinking and a few who drank heavily. But my colleague had committed the unforgivable sin. He had failed to sober up for the mission. As a result, he was now face to face with what he really was: a well-educated, highly trained, glib, good looking, reckless drunk.

Though he had not chosen the war, he had made certain choices. His career was finished. The spiritual void in his life, which his technical background would not let him acknowledge, had been filled with activities, thrills, things! And God's grace had been ignored.

And so it is today. There are those of us who have landed gear up . . . and there are those of us who are about to. Life does have a way of getting our attention, or at least pointing out our inattention and asking us pointblank what we want from it.

Lord, make me willing.
With Christ, our attitudes, our values, and ultimately our behavior—so easily influenced by that spiritual vacuum— can be brought into harmony with something so much more

than a double-tongued saxophone, a needle, a flask, or even something as innocent as the demands of "the bottom line." Grace changes what we want . . . if we'll let it. And that's the problem. It's a little frightening because we think we know what we want! In fact, our culture admires a man of destiny, a man who knows what he wants and goes after it. And that's fine. But individually, we all find ourselves from time to time confronted with the need to make a choice . . . a change. But for some reason, we dare not admit it.

Over the years, when I hesitated to face some necessary spiritual surgery, I prayed, "Lord, make me willing to be willing." And He answers. Not right away, and not without some struggle, but He answers. Paul offers us hope when he reminds us, "It is God who works in you to will and to act according to his good purpose" (Philippians 2:13).

We can actually get to the point where God's desire for us directly influences our desire, and we find the discipline to live accordingly. Grace deals with our will, redirecting our efforts to assume full responsibility for our lives before God. Grace touches what we want and lifts us out of the spiritual death that surrounds us, the vacuum, and leads us into new life. As Paul said, "If, by the trespass of the one man, death reigned through that one man, how much more will those who receive God's abundant provision of grace and of the gift of righteousness reign in life through the one man, Jesus Christ." (Romans 5:17). But will we receive it? Will we accept God's gift?

The freedom flight

I'll never forget a discussion I had with one of my colleagues. When I told him how much I was looking forward to finishing my tour and getting on the "freedom flight" to go home, he very emphatically reminded me that "this mess is the only war we've got!" Suffering from a good case of career induced blindness, he went on to say that if a man was going to "make a name for himself," it would have to be here. I probed a little deeper to see if he was serious. He was.

I had heard about people like this, but he was the first one I actually ran across in the flesh. For him the war was only a means to his ends of personal glory and promotion. "Besides," he said, "Bangkok is a real hot spot—all the action a guy could want!" And so on.

Though his attitude was by far the minority opinion, it did bring up a very real issue. Do we want the alternative that is offered? There is a freedom flight, but have we lost interest in the game we're currently playing? Or do we feel that there's still something in it for us if we could only figure out how to manipulate it to our advantage? Are we tired enough of "Bangkok" and the escapism of our day or broken enough by our own definition of life to want something totally new? Have we allowed the Lord to make us willing to *receive* that amazing grace?

When we first arrived in the war zone we didn't think about the freedom flight all that much because we were caught up in the new, the different, the adventure—and just plain survival. What we had heard about during training— missiles, antiaircraft fire, combat fatigue, timetables, rendez- vous points—was no longer abstract theory. We were sur- rounded by the veterans, the survivors of a hundred or more missions, who were more than willing to interact with the "new guys," and even fly with us, if necessary, just to help us learn the ropes. We didn't have time to think about the freedom flight. Other things seemed to be so much more important, so much more crucial to our very survival.

However, as time went on, those of us who survived began to place our focus increasingly on the freedom flight. We would even hesitantly allow ourselves to speculate on what the future might hold on the other side of the war. The freedom flight! We functioned, and then in our more private moments we wondered: What will it be like? The freedom flight! When we lost yet another friend, our rotation date to the States seemed to move further away and the weeks passed more slowly. But in spite of it all, there was always the freedom flight!

The closer that day came, the larger that bird loomed on the horizon. By then, we had seen and done. We had laughed and cried, loved and lost. At best, it had been a mixed bag, where a lifetime was compressed into a few short months, leaving us without the shadow of a doubt that there just had to be something else . . . something more. The symbol of that hope would crystallize in the mind. The freedom flight!

Though I had only a month to go, the war raged on. Hanoi Harbor was mined. Heretofore routine reconnaissance missions were now stumbling upon very lucrative military targets: the storage and staging areas of the offensive, truck parks, ammunition, fuel depots, and occasional troop concentrations. Neither Hanoi nor Washington were going to lose what proved to be the final major military showdown of that undeclared war between them. Both sides pulled out the stops. Great risks were taken, and losses continued to mount.

But every day the freedom flight took off with two hundred more on board. Though it was just a small fraction of the total number of combatants, within a couple of hours many happy men would be somewhere over the Pacific completely out of the war zone. A few hours more and they would be touching down at Hickham Air Force Base, Hawaii! The U.S. of A.! After a brief layover, they would continue on to the West Coast. Having set foot once again in the land of peace and prosperity, they would gather their luggage, chat just one more time with their buddies about the promised "reunion" (which would never happen), and take their well-earned leaves to fly on home to mom, the kids, or their best girl . . . to try to forget it all.

Taking the freedom flight represented the essence of Paul's teaching on obedience: that God is much more interested in where we want to go than in where we have been! Christ has already died for where we have been and has liberated God's grace for where we want to go. Our response should be found in a desire to turn it around—and follow through. Repentance. To take just a few small steps! God's freedom flight.

In his opening argument in Romans 6, Paul exclaims "Don't you know . . . ?" Don't you know that the opportunity and the power to live an alternative lifestyle exists? Don't you know that no matter how much you think you need to follow your impulses, there is a higher motivation that has now been made available to you? We already know in our hearts what is necessary. Obedience is not a mystery. Our conscience, with the help of our friends, can make it clear. God has not asked us to do the unreasonable or harsh by asking us to separate from sin. As Paul explains, "We died to sin; how can we live in it any longer?" (Romans 6:2).

What is sin?

The theologians tell us that sin in its purest sense is rebellion against God. Sin presumes to know better, but, in the process, winds up reaching for something ultimately self-defeating and unworthy. In striving for more than God intended, sin winds up forcing us to live with so much less. Paul reminds us, "Although they claimed to be wise, they became fools and exchanged the glory of the immortal God for images made to look like mortal man . . . " (Romans 1:22).

Sin exchanges God's plan for a lesser one. Oh, it looks pretty enough and glittery enough. But in reaching for it, sin trades love for lust, integrity for "success," truthfulness for expediency, people for possessions, and purpose for something as fleeting as pleasure. In overreaching itself, sin falls into the abyss of vanity, perhaps the most pervasive symptom of spiritual death in our modern society.

Vanity and death

After his gear-up landing, my colleague was grounded by the old man and placed under house arrest until a board could be convened to study the matter and make recommendations. At first he was sorry, then angry when he realized his excuses no longer cut it with the old man. Having gone so far as to polish his boots, he tried to recapture the crisp professional look that his time in the war zone had long since eroded away. In conversation, he would allude to pressures as though he were the only one experiencing them. Blaming the war, or others, his inability to face himself was glaringly obvious to everyone.

And then he got quiet. We can only imagine what went through his mind. We can only guess how many times he asked himself, "What happened?" At what point did he lose the focus on his future and his daily responsibility to it? It's probably safe to assume that he cried. That the strut had been knocked out of him, we could all attest to. Flying had been his life, and now he was facing the consequences of having destroyed it.

Vanity is paying more for something than it's worth. For him, a promising career was gone, not because he couldn't have it but because he wanted something else more. He traded what he could have for what he couldn't—the illusion. Like many of us, he made the painful discovery that he could not go back. For we don't realize we're trapped in the vanity of this life until what little gain has been derived in the short-term vanishes like a mirage in light of long-term losses. Broken, we're left wondering if the laughter we hear is all that is left of our own conscience. As we catch a glimpse of ourselves, Christ's piercing question probes the emptiness. "What good is it for a man to gain the whole world, yet forfeit his soul?" (Mark 8:36).

Given time, vanity leads to death's purposeless wandering—the curse of Cain. It's existing but not really living; searching, but never finding. It's even risking, only to find loss—bitterness, confusion, and the constant grinding tension of emotional and relational bankruptcy. It's knowing that something's missing, that we have been made for so much more, and realizing that somehow, somewhere, we've betrayed that higher calling. Lost it! And though we can remember what it was like, an invisible flaming sword seems to stand between us and what used to be, barring us from it, forever. Spiritual death is trying to find life where God never intended us to live: "east of Eden." We cannot escape the consequences of our choices, and life *will* force us to choose.

So why not choose life? Paul goes on to teach us how.

Dead reckoning

"Count yourselves dead to sin but alive to God in Christ Jesus. Therefore do not let sin reign in your mortal body so that you obey its evil desires" (Romans 6:11-12).

Dead reckoning! That's what the pilots call it. Its history stems from the barnstorming days when the instrumentation in the early biplanes was quite primitive. There were no radio beacons or other navigational aids to home in on. In a fog, under icing conditions, or when a pilot accidentally flew off the map, all he had left to bring himself, the mail, or his passengers safely home was his best guess based on his experience and proven luck. His reckoning. If he was wrong, well. . . .

As Christians, we are subject to another kind of dead

reckoning. Though the translations vary, the idea is clear: "Count yourselves dead to sin . . . consider yourselves dead to sin . . . reckon yourselves dead to sin." There is an irrevocable decision to be made, a step of personal accountability to be taken, personal responsibilities to be assumed. God will not remove the burden of mature adulthood from us. But, He has promised to help us bear it and, in the process, experience His grace.

That's the way it was with the freedom flight. There were those who, like my colleague, were convinced that they could still personally benefit from the chaos. That the game could still be won and that they were just the type to win it. The extent of self-deception involved in this reasoning process can only be speculated on. However, it was obvious that the "pleasures of Bangkok" made the game palatable no matter how faulty his reckoning. Knowing that the freedom flight existed, he chose to ignore it, at least for a while.

However, as I said goodbye to another buddy who was leaving, I was indelibly marked when he said, "Just a few small steps up that ramp and I'll be home." What a statement of faith! He had implicit confidence in the competence of the crew, the reliability of the navigational equipment, and the structural integrity of that aircraft. "Just a few small steps." And so it is with Christ. Will we yield to the process? When we see an area of discord in our lives that separates us from God, will we do some dead reckoning and yield to Him? No alternative is possible without turning our back on the chaos. This is the essence of repentance.

For, we cannot escape the consequences of our choices. What we "yield to" ultimately becomes our master. The most difficult truth to swallow is that we will all surrender to something. Something or someone will dominate us. It's only a question of who, what, and when. Given time, we all become slaves. As Paul says, "Don't you know that when you offer yourselves to someone to obey him as slaves, you are slaves to the one whom you obey—whether you are slaves to sin, which leads to death, or to obedience, which leads to righteousness" (Romans 6:16).

Though all the soldiers on those freedom flights were impatient to get home, they were still facing a twenty-four hour journey. But they were at least assured that they were on their way. And so it can be for the Christian. Though home with Christ is still a long way off, as we take the few small steps that conscience demands, we, too, can know that we are on our way. The significance of simple obedience was not fully clear to me until I reflected upon it in light of an experience I had one day when I was caught in the clouds in a crippled aircraft.

CHAPTER EIGHT

Flying by Instruments

Trust in the LORD with all your heart and
lean not on your own understanding; in all your
ways acknowledge him, and he will make your
paths straight.
(Proverbs 3:5-6)

■

God's commandments . . . conscience . . . sin . . . and a war. There was that constant tension between my private world and the world that surrounded me. In the midst of it all was the growing desire to walk a "straight path." Choices! Choices that affected only me, and choices that affected others. In this case, it was often a choice between life or death. Daily, I faced that incessant tension between what is going on inside a man and how well he relates to his environment, the essence of integrity.

Why was it so hard to attain? What could we count on in the struggle to attain it? Everything around me seemed to be spiritual quicksand. Truth, once again, had been war's first victim. It seemed that if a missile or flak didn't get me, the half-truths would. For when men are far from their country, their roots, things become a little fuzzy. In trying to clarify what the truth is, they're prone to believe anything that will give a little comfort or hope . . . or respite from trying to figure it all out.

But that brings us back to the question. What can we count on in the struggle for integrity? Who are our allies? Or, as a pilot might say, what instruments do we have to fly through the clouds of the human condition?

Approaching Da Nang, one of our largest bases situated on the Vietnamese coast, the plane was shaking from battle damage. But I was also shaking. I had just heard the rescue team cry out, "A ball of flames! The chopper's down! We lost them!" Sitting behind me with all the navigation equipment and laser technology at his fingertips was the navigator. Both of us were stone silent. We had tried so hard. We had done the job, or so we thought. They should have been able to get them out. I couldn't get it out of my mind.

As the vibrations increased, we were shocked back to present realities. We'd have to put off our mourning until later. If we didn't get down soon, we, too, would have to eject and the rescue problems would only be compounded. So, I declared an emergency.

"Da Nang control, this is Nail. I'm on your 320 radial at 38 miles, flight level 9000. I'm declaring an emergency . . . request priority clearance and an in-route descent to an ILS final approach, GCA backup. How copy?"

"Copy 5-by, Nail, but runways are closed due to thunderstorms. Ceiling's zero . . . visibility's a quarter mile. Request you divert. How copy?"

"Copy, but diversion impossible. Give me a vector to intercept the ILS"

"Roger, turn left heading 120, descend to 6000."

And so it went. "Normal-normal," as we used to say. Emergencies were the norm of the war zone. As the navigator cranked the appropriate numbers into the instruments, before my eyes appeared a representation of the runway and our position with respect to it.

Our aircraft was wounded and in the clouds. The rain was pelting the wind-screen and I couldn't see twenty feet in front of me. However, as we descended, both of us were confident. For, on the ground there were signals being transmitted to the five radios and three navigation aids on board the aircraft. My eyes were glued in a constant cross-check to those lifesaving instruments, which were interpreting the signals for us: altitude, airspeed, glide slope, and center line of the runway. Though I was not able to see, the wonders of technology had extended my vision. I could see the invisible! Home base and safety were within sight.

Flying by instruments

There comes a moment when a man knows that he's a pilot. He just knows it! However, it takes time. In the early phases, there is study, and training in the simulators, those million-dollar cockpits that never leave the ground. Then there are those daily flights that force you to apply what you've learned. You go through the rigors and the motions until gradually you develop instincts—unconscious application of your newly acquired knowledge. But that doesn't mean you can now fly by the seat of your pants! For, one of the most important of those instincts is the constant cross-check of your instruments, particularly when you are "in the weather." This is a point the instructor pilots made painfully clear.

The course on instrument flying at Randolph Air Force Base began with a gripping documentary film on an actual aircraft accident. You were taken into the radar control center where you overheard the dialogue between the ground controller, staring into his large radar scope, and an inexperienced pilot caught in the clouds. Running low on fuel, this amateur needed to get down in a hurry. Apparently he'd taken his family on a little Sunday ride in the sky when the weather abruptly changed, reducing his visibility to zero in the clouds, rain, lightning, and characteristic turbulence of a plains state "thunder bumper."

The tension mounted as the ground controller tried to vector the man and his unsuspecting family through the clouds, which grew more and more ominous and impenetrable. As we heard the strain in the pilot's voice, we began to imagine how he must have felt. How shocking it must have been to realize that he was not qualified to handle the situation and that the lives of his family were hanging in the balance. By now it was clear: he didn't know how to read his instruments. Literally unable to distinguish between up or down due to transverse G-forces and the blinding storm, he began following his untrained senses and tried to "right" the plane on several occasions, only aggravating the situation.

Finally, the radar controller screamed at him, "Release the controls! Release the controls!" For, he knew that nearly all the light planes in the private aviation industry will fly themselves . . . more or less. They've even been known to fly themselves out of a spin. But, in this case, it was too late. All we heard at that point were high-pitched screams as the pilot keyed the mike one more time and yelled, "Help! Help! Help! Help! We're out of control! We're out of control!" There was only silence . . . and the voice of the distraught controller trying to raise them yet one more time on the radios, but to no avail.

We were dazed, nonplussed!

As the film came to an end, the lights came on and the instructor took the platform. "Now that I have your attention. . . ." Then he went on to describe the course. Admittedly, it was a brutal way to start. But it was absolutely vital when you consider that the audience he was addressing would someday be carrying passengers, cargo, or—bombs. However, he didn't stop there. After some more preliminaries, he took us into the lab and introduced us to "the chair."

Looking like a cross between modern art and a flying saucer, the chair was one of these space-age wonders designed to humble young pilot aspirants even further. Sitting in the middle of a labyrinth of tubes, servos, and gyros was a chair that would freely tumble and turn at the slightest touch of the hand. Attached to it was a control stick similar to what one would find in a fighter cockpit.

Taking an unsuspecting volunteer, the instructor seated him in the chair and blindfolded him. Slowly spinning the chair to the left, he asked the pilot to "correct" his attitude by using the control stick to bring the chair back to its original position. Having touched the chair only once, the instructor stepped back—and the comedy began.

Having only the sensory inputs of the fluid in his inner ear to give him a feel for motion and direction, the "pilot" started chasing himself all over the sky. Swinging the chair back to the right and then to the left again, he eventually leaned on his right side and swore that he was in the vertical. And so it went. This continued for several minutes, as the instructor queried the pilot on occasion with respect to his concept of straight and level. With each response, it was all the observers could do to hold back the laughter.

If it hadn't been so pathetic, it would have been hilarious. But when the blindfold was finally removed, the shock on his face was duly recorded by all. We now knew why a family had perished—and why we were not yet pilots. A pilot has to learn not to trust his own "leanings." What feels right, just isn't. A man is not a pilot until he can trust his *instruments*!

And so it was for me that fateful day in that vibrating plane, and for the man sitting behind me in complete trust. As the vibrations increased and as the lightning became the only light in a dark, sunless sky, we threaded our aircraft through the clouds. The ground controller monitored our approach on the radar, ready to give us any assistance we might need in our emergency. Fire trucks were standing by the runway, and a chase helicopter filled with fire-fighting equipment and mer. ready to cut us out of the wreckage were also prepared in case we did not make the runway.

Though it had been a long day—too long!—and though we were now breathing a little heavily, our training paid off. There were moments when the confusion in the clouds could have been fatal, times when all our senses seemed to indicate that the instruments were lying, moments when confusion could have reigned, making panic and pilot error inevitable. But I had been trained to trust the instruments. And I did. Making the minute corrections necessary to stay on the glide slope, I knew that if the plane held together, we'd make it.

As we broke out of the clouds a hundred feet off the runway and in a perfect attitude for landing, all that remained to do was to ease back the power and the stick and let her settle onto the runway. As the emergency vehicles approached with their blaring sirens and flashing lights, I knew they would not be necessary. I had trusted the instruments. I was a pilot—and that was the day I knew it for sure.

And so it is with God. He has endowed us with spiritual instruments to get us through the storm clouds of the human condition. The question is: Do we know how to interpret them? And, having received the message, will we trust it with our very lives? This is the essence of faith.

The instruments of faith

The instruments had gotten us through the clouds! However, during the preflight check, the instruments had to be verified by placing the compass on true north and stabilizing the gyros with respect to the known and proven horizon. And so it is with our instruments in the daily struggle for integrity.

Our conscience, given its ability to seek out God, must nevertheless be trained in the ethical implications of the law. This process, which continues throughout our lives, tunes us to our spiritual north pole and helps us get stabilized with respect to the sure horizon. Though today we seem to relish the thought that our Puritan ancestors left us with a restrictive conscience that needs to be thrown off in order to experience growth, the apostle Paul makes the meaning of the law very clear when he says, "Indeed I would not have known what sin was except through the law. For I would not have known what coveting really was if the law had not said, 'Do not covet'" (Romans 7:7).

Without the law to sensitize our conscience in light of God's design, we're without instruments as we fly into the clouds of mere human opinion. We've no true north, no stable horizon to focus on. Without our instruments, we're literally at the mercy of the storm, tempted to add our pilot-induced error to an already dangerous situation. In other words, we misinterpret the input, thus leading a vain life, if not a disastrous one.

But our conscience can help us make the necessary distinctions before it's too late. Just as a pilot must cross-check his instruments continually in order to make necessary corrections and course changes, so must a Christian heed the warnings of the law and the conscience. When something in us begins to speak—or shout!—a choice has to be made.

Sometimes all we may have is a feeling that something is "not right" with a situation. Though faith by its very nature is full of risks and unanswered questions, integrity should not be. Even in a war—if it's doubtful, it's dirty.

The limits of conscience

So, when we speak of drug abuse, for example, we're speaking of one of the more obvious manifestations of human error. We have to hope that its victims see their situation as it really is, showing that they've learned their lesson by subscribing to a new lifestyle. If they don't particularly want to talk about "getting religion," then let's just talk about "getting smart." But, let's talk.

However, the apostle Paul was an eminently respectable and very religious man. From the outside, there was probably very little you could criticize him for. Nevertheless, on the inside Paul was in turmoil. Why? "For in my inner being I delight in God's law; but I see another law at work in the members of my body, waging war against the law of my mind and making me a prisoner of the law of sin at work within my members" (Romans 7:22-23).

A war was being waged within him. God's law had honed and refined his conscience since his youth. His compass and gyros had passed the preflight inspection. As a critical scholar of the prophets and the traditions, Paul knew what to do and when. However, for that reason he fell into the trap of the religious man. He became convinced, as many of us do, that he could attain some sort of righteousness in the eyes of God. Paul felt compelled to obey—in order to be saved. He wanted to improve his standing, his merit before the Almighty, and somehow, someway, make God his debtor to the point where his salvation would be earned and assured. As it was for his fellow Jews, he unconsciously wanted his salvation to be something he could be proud of! So he worked at it.

But in the process he discovered that though conscience is a fairly good guide of what God wants of us, he needed something more if he was to successfully live for Him. For he was being harassed by an ever-present enemy. Try as he may, he failed . . . and failed . . . and failed again. Though his conscience affirmed that the law was righteous, he found he just couldn't reach that high! Why? Because there was, just as real as the risen Christ he had encountered and now tried to serve, a treacherous enemy who would twist and contort the most noble aspects of that service, making him feel as though he were a prisoner caught in a constant struggle . . . a war.

Facing Paul was an enemy just as implacable in the spiritual domain as the one we faced in Nam.

CHAPTER NINE
Enemies of Faith

*Our struggle is not against flesh and blood, but
against . . . the powers of this dark world and
against the spiritual forces of evil. . . .*
(Ephesians 6:12)

■

As we approached the target in loose combat formation, a
telltale trail of snow-white smoke pointed the finger of death
at the aircraft just a few hundred yards away from me.
"Break right!" I screamed over the radios. "SAM! SAM!
Break right!" But, I was too late. I watched helplessly as the
missile corrected on their evasive maneuver and continued
tracking them until everything vaporized in a brilliant red-
hot fireball. Another crew was gone. No parachutes! No calls
on Guard frequency! Nothing! Just that dull orange cloud,
destruction's remnant, lingering where they once were . . .
and fear.

Shaken . . . I was shaking in a cold sweat . . . and awoke
from my nightmare screaming, "SAM! SAM! . . . Break . . .
right . . . Break . . . !" But my voice trailed off as my mind
crawled slowly back into consciousness and the realization
that for the moment, at least, I was safe. My roommate

switched on the light, and after a few frustrating, sleep-filled expressions, rolled over to leave me to my embarrassed silence. Nothing to get excited about—*he* was the one who had "the shakes" the night before.

Staring at the ceiling, I reflected on a little bit of everything—and nothing. Random images flashed across my mind: missiles, flak, a chopper that went down, home, the freedom flight, and the eerie sense of being "mission essential personnel" to a war that apparently was no longer essential.

Somewhere in the middle of it all was God. *God!* If, as Paul said, taking that spiritual freedom flight was so simple, then why was it so hard? If it's just a matter of taking a few steps, why can't we seem to do it? What forces align themselves against us? What enemies are we facing? These things I wondered, but not for long. As the sun rose, so did I . . . for the next mission.

We had to stop them! But in the process of trying, we had to come to realize just how tenacious the enemy was. We all knew now just how much the North Vietnamese were willing to sacrifice for "their" ideal and how little, by comparison, those in the South were willing to sacrifice for "ours." And in that tenacity and conviction was found all the difference.

Democracy and capitalism meant a great deal . . . to us. Democracy! Our glorious ideal had been forged in the furnace of European history and then exported to the new world, wrapped in religious zeal. Uninhibited in its early development by foreign interference, it was nurtured and grew to the point where it could successfully resist a king and his armies. We were free!

With that freedom came capitalism: the freedom of the marketplace, the democratization of the means of production and distribution. What could be more universal than that? What could be more egalitarian than that? Why wouldn't someone want to sacrifice to successfully pass it on to their children? And so on. And so I sincerely believed. And so did many others—but not the South Vietnamese.

It seems incredibly naive to be writing these phrases now, when we better appreciate the mysteries of the Orient with its Taoist world view. In its essence, Taoism states that we should all lead a simple and natural life, going with the flow of the universe. There is an element of fatalism in this mind-set. The people were merely like the grass, having to bend with the winds of the times. Only this way could they keep their higher consciousness intact—their Tao. Only this way could they and their now sacred family plot of land, the one thing in this life that they valued, be passed on to posterity.

So, at the village level, the person armed with this world view passively survived. First it was the Khmers, then the Chinese, then the French, then the Japanese, then the French again, and now us. Though I still think we can say that our motives were honestly different from the other armies that had marched across those sacred yet scarred family plots, to the Vietnamese we looked the same. It was inevitable.

Their recent history had been little more than that of being exploited by colonial powers operating on the very principles of capitalism that I unconsciously lauded in my mind. It's strange, but the education that these same colonizers provided proved to be the means by which the Vietnamese ultimately prevailed. Learning of Marx and Lenin, whose ideals also spoke of putting the means of production and distribution in the hands of the people, gave them the philosophic basis to reject both a passive Taoism and the active incursion of yet another foreign power.

So the debate raged. Were they full-fledged communists who, as part of a worldwide cartel controlled by Moscow, were trying to criminally abort the embryo of democracy now finally implanted on the Asian mainland? Of this, some were fully convinced. Or, were they just patriots trying to throw off the yoke of colonialism to fulfill their manifest destiny under one banner and a very popular leader by the name of Ho Chi Minh? In the sixties, it was still too soon to say. So the troops were sent. But as time passed, both military and political positions hardened.

Division at home over this issue led our president, one known to be tough on communism, to begin speaking of "peace with honor." He wanted to get us out of a no-win situation. "Shuttle-diplomacy" was becoming a well-known phrase. Secret talks were taking place. However, while the debate raged and the hometown editorialists speculated on the outcome, in Vietnam, the two opposing world views collided. For us—the soldiers, pilots, and sailors—the orders remained the same. The sad reality persisted. Until further notice, we had to stop them!

A thousand miles of tunnels, which they had carved out of the earth and rock, hid entire supply depots, truck parks, training centers, and staging areas for the offensive we had been facing at heavy cost since that fateful Easter Sunday. Convinced that time and justice were on his side, "Charlie," as we called him, threw himself into the massive coordinated attacks that overwhelmed the South Vietnamese armies . . . a harbinger of things to come. Though Charlie was hit, and hit hard, again and again, he kept coming. He was a relentless foe. I have never met a veteran who did not have respect for Charlie. The enemy.

The struggle

We face an enemy of another kind when we speak of the struggle for spiritual growth. Try as we may to take the necessary steps to a whole new life, we find that we feel openly attacked or harassed. But, it's always been that way.

As it was with Joshua, so also with us: the Promised Land does not come without a fight. Having been delivered from Pharaoh and having finally, a generation later, decided to act on the promise and carve out a new life, Joshua and his people were not without daily struggles, pitched battles, and the need for constant diligence. Obedience was the order of the day. Though God loved His children unconditionally, even after a generation of disobedience it was also clear that His promises were conditional. The full potential of His children would only be found in struggle—and faith. "If you carefully observe all these commands I am giving you to follow—to love the LORD your God, to walk in all his ways and to hold fast to him—then the LORD will drive out all these nations before you, and you will dispossess nations larger and stronger than you" (Deuteronomy 11:22-23).

Faced with a new life in the Promised Land, Israel was also faced with nations to be "dispossessed." Enemies. Some lost hope as they saw strong fortified cities filled with giants standing between them and their place in the sun. Others, like Joshua, heard the voice of God. He knew that opposing world views, religions, and values could eventually undermine everything God was trying to do for and through His people.

As I studied this story, I realized that it's the same for our personal lives. Though the potential for fulfillment in Christ exists, there are areas of profound resistance to the will of God in our lives, areas yet to be encountered. These areas must be overcome, "dispossessed," if we are to grow and eventually possess all that God has for us in this life. For even as Christians, we have attitudes, values, and behavior based on nothing more profound than the egotism of a materialistic society or the passion of the moment. Like it or not, we're faced with a struggle against enemies: our own flesh, a world that is hostile to the revelation of God, and a subtle yet powerful enemy that has been seducing man since that fateful day in the garden so long ago.

Paul introduces us to what that struggle actually feels like when he says, "I do not understand what I do. For what I want to do I do not do, but what I hate I do. . . . For I have the desire to do what is good, but I cannot carry it out. For what I do is not the good I want to do—this I keep on doing. Now if I do what I do not want to do, it is no longer I who do it, but it is sin living in me that does it" (Romans 7:15-20).

Paul was not being morbidly introspective here, nor was he suffering from a neurosis. He was honestly and humbly acknowledging that he could not live up to his own convictions. Can we be that honest with ourselves? Here was a man known for his rigor and self-discipline. Nevertheless, Paul knew that *he* was the problem.

By stating that the principle of sin and death was a vital part of his own existence, Paul was not sidestepping the issue of personal responsibility as some would think. Rather, he was taking the necessary first step in dealing with it. He was owning up to the fact that in spite of his impressive religious trappings, he was a sinner—no better than anyone else. So Paul discovered that he lacked the power to live up to the expectations of his own conscience and the even higher dictates of his religious training. And it was profoundly frustrating to him.

So, I discovered that Paul knew how I felt! In the midst of struggling with my own concept of integrity, I was encouraged to realize that choices were not really clear and simple for Paul. He was one of us. He struggled. He failed. He wrestled with his own flesh, motives, desires, and goals. And in his confession, we see the humility of a learner who says, "When I want to do good, evil is right there with me" (Romans 7:21). Brutally honest, Paul shows us the nature of repentance when he cries out, "Who will rescue me from this body of death?" Or, in other words, "Who will save me—from me? Why is it that I not only do what is ultimately self-defeating but I also actively avoid that which is ultimately beneficial?"

The man or the environment?

Is the answer to this question about why I do what I do found in man or in his environment? Sociologists, historians, and people in the street have been debating for years whether the man makes the society or the society makes the man. And the debate will go on. For though we see that Paul clearly declared that the fault was with him, in another text, however, he warned against the influence of the environment— "the world": "Do not conform any longer to the pattern of this world, but be transformed by the renewing of your mind. Then you will be able to test and approve what God's will is—his good, pleasing and perfect will" (Romans 12:2).

There are pressures. "Patterns." Conformity is expected. This is the nature of our world. Therefore, we must understand that one of the enemies of spiritual growth is the old pattern, the old ways, and the pervasive influences that surround us. It is very little wonder that God must lead us into a desert before He can grant us the Promised Land. It's only in the desert, far from the old half-truths, that old habits and patterns die and new ones are born—based on integrity.

But just what is it about our world that is so displeasing to God?

The world

The world is the enemy of faith only to the extent that our participation in the world is noncritical. "Because everyone else is doing it" has never been the rallying cry of the faithful in Christ. The corrupt world has little to do with its original creation by God. It has, rather, to do with man, the creature that God has made responsible for it. We are responsible for the *why*—the motivations—of what we do.

The apostle John gives us a strong warning about not immersing ourselves in the ways of the world. "Do not love the world or anything in the world. If anyone loves the world, the love of the Father is not in him. For everything in the world—the cravings of sinful man, the lust of his eyes and the boasting of what he has and does—comes not from the Father but from the world. The world and its desires pass away, but the man who does the will of God lives forever" (1 John 2:15-17).

What makes the world go 'round? John says that the driving force is "lust," or "cravings." The creation is still filled with much of its original God-given potential, but the issue is how we go about harnessing it. This passage in 1 John gives us the three basic areas of confusion in which we can lose this potential, even our humanity, unless we find the grace in Christ to break out, to take the freedom flight and recapture it.

Passion—In this fallen world, man is vulnerable to "the lust of the flesh," or "cravings." Legitimate longings and appetites become twisted and eventually perverted by a godless world view. For if God is not there, then our appetites become our substitute god. They focus us and govern our choices in such a way that we become their slaves, and others become their prey. The god of our wants and the lord of our needs lead us on. And no matter how intelligent we are, our energies become channeled in such a way that even with a God-given potential for so much more, we end up settling for so much less. This is the siren of passion.

Possessions—The "lust of the eyes" speaks of the god of this high-tech world: materialism. The most difficult word in the *world* to define is "enough"! When is enough really enough? Throughout the Scriptures, we are taught the importance of contentment and simplicity. We are warned about the potential trap of materialism.

"Just a little bit more" does not speak of life's necessities. It speaks rather of lifestyle. But when Christ taught us to pray for "our daily bread," He was speaking of necessities: food, clothing, and shelter. These are the elements of a simpler lifestyle, which He Himself modeled. We can normally expect God to respond to our need for life's necessities, but whether or not we should expect Him to respond to what we see to be our rightful place in the American dream is the subject of much debate.

For though Jesus Himself had little more than the basic necessities of this life, we're forced to ask if there has ever been a life more worthy than His. And perhaps that is the question to guide us through this maze of materialism that surrounds us: Just what *is* worthy?

God certainly does not measure a man by some "bottom line," and I think He probably reserves the right to judge someone who does. Our own lust for more, bigger, and better, though certainly helpful in driving the economy, is of little help in nourishing the soul. Eventually the impoverishment of our wealth overwhelms us as we realize we've learned the price of everything and the value of nothing.

Position—"The pride of life" indicates a lust for position or power. In our high-tech culture, what one does is very important. As a matter of fact, it often seems as though our position is to be equated with our identity, and even our worth. For a Christian, merely being a child of God just isn't enough anymore. As my colleague said, "A man can really make a name for himself" in the right war. So, we play the game: credentials, titles, and introductions to the right people. And so on.

However, a god-filled lifestyle produces an empty

life—because the real God is not in it. It may not be church-less, but the focus of its very existence is temporal. When the soul feeds on the world and everything worldly, all creativity goes into the quest for upward mobility and the public display of "success" without critical concern for the brevity of life and what is essential because of it.

Eventually, however, we can no longer fool ourselves. We see the lust—its destructive results and the patterns that foster it—and ask, "Why? Is this all there is? Why can't I break out of it? Why am I surrendering to it?"

It's not until we've come to this point in our personal odyssey that we are ready to face another enemy: the force behind it all. If we attribute the conscience of man and the good that it inspires within us to the God who is love, then logic demands that all that the conscience decries as evil also has an ultimate source. Something—no, some*one*—is tug-ging at the strings, using the passions, possessions, and posi-tions in this world to seduce and to blind those who refuse to believe that He is even there.

His strategy is simple. But, I didn't understand it until I sensed how lonely a man could feel flying through the clouds.

CHAPTER TEN

The Primary Enemy

We do not have a high priest who is unable to
sympathize with our weaknesses, but we have one
who has been tempted in every way, just as we are—
yet was without sin. Let us then approach the throne
of grace with confidence, so that we may receive
mercy and find grace to help us in our time of need.
(Hebrews 4:15-16)

∎

Alone. That's probably the toughest feeling to overcome when you're "in the soup," pilots' jargon for bad weather. That sad day, the day the chopper went down and we were heading back to base in a crippled aircraft, I knew I had to master myself if I was ever to master the situation. Fighting back the rage and frustration, knowing that if I cried at all it would have to be later, perhaps years later, I went about methodically applying the proven emergency procedures. But, in spite of those professional reflexes, there was still the unknown. Would the plane hold together? What was the extent of the damage? Were the instruments still reliable? And, for that matter, was I?

For weeks, machines and men had been pushed to the limit, and now I found myself in a tropical thunderstorm with nowhere to go but to a runway that was socked in. Even though the base was also threatened by an imminent attack, I refused to think about it. I forced myself to calm down. The instruments! They were my only link to reality. I had to trust the instruments! Of that I was sure. For, years earlier, during the course on instrument flying, I had learned to understand . . .

Invisible signals

"Today, gentlemen," the major began, "we are going to cover the reason why even the most qualified pilots can become so confused that they might be forced to eject in order to save their own lives. We're not talking about battle damage or equipment failure. Confusion in the cockpit can reign at any time when the pilot refuses to acknowledge his human limits." Then he calmly went on to illustrate his point by telling the kind of true stories that left his youthful audience convinced that merely being human can be fatal.

Thoroughly discussing the limits of pilot performance that day, we learned that the body simply cannot sense, process, or measure certain kinds of stimuli that are nevertheless there. Energy, for example, can only be sensed during a turn, or phases of acceleration and deceleration. In normal flight, as in normal travel in any other vehicle, such as a car, one is simply not aware of energy unless, as with an accident, it suddenly changes.

The same is true for the invisible radio and television waves surrounding us with thousands of signals daily. We just aren't aware of them. Yet in our technological age no one would ever doubt their existence, for we can prove it with the mere flick of a switch. Having extended our senses with the use of receivers, we can benefit from the ideas and images being transmitted. Though these waves are not commonly understood, they are commonly accepted as a fact of modern life. We live every day with the visible effects of the invisible, the proof of an unseen reality.

Between two realities

For the pilot, an unseen world is the very basis of instrument flying. The instruments give only indications of the greater reality that lies beyond—a home base and safety. But these indications have to become the *ultimate* reference point if the pilot is to survive. Though the instruments themselves are visible and interpreted accordingly, all that goes into making them trustworthy is invisible. And there's the problem.

When what the pilot "feels" to be straight and level is no longer reinforced by the instruments, internal conflict is experienced. This leaves him caught in the tension of being forced to choose between two realities. One reality demands that he deny his feelings and trust his instruments. The other, however, employs his sensory organs to demand that the plane be "righted" according to how he feels. The tension can be quite frustrating, particularly if the pilot is alone in the cockpit, surrounded by a storm. If the pilot fails to resolve it, even the most experienced could be forced to "hit the silk"—parachuting, and thus abandoning the plane. Though this certainly represented the height of embarrassment for the professional and often announced the end of an otherwise promising career, nevertheless, at least he lived to tell about it.

One such story was recorded to impress upon future pilots just how tough facing this tension could be. Caught at night in an electrical storm and trying to resolve his confusion in a cramped cockpit, an experienced pilot humbly told the camera what it was like to feel "all alone up there." Those of us watching were moved as he repeated that word over and over and over again. "Alone!" And feeling alone, more than anything else, was the cause of his panic. Penetrating those ominous clouds, his plane began to flow with static discharge. Though this was a normal enough phenomenon, it drove him to distraction, blocking his interpretation of the instruments and causing him to eventually fail. Fortunately, his parachute didn't.

After the film, the instructor allowed a moment of silence. No one stirred. When he was convinced that the film had thoroughly impacted his audience, he went on to cover in detail what accident investigations had revealed to date about human perception—and pilot error. The truth was brutal, and his summary was simple. Faced with these two realities—the one of our instruments and the other of our feelings—we placed ourselves in danger if "the correct stimulus lacked sufficient strength to convince the pilot to follow it." This was a polite way of saying that if the pilot failed to keep his eyes within the cockpit and glued to the instruments, he could confuse himself by trying to find some reference point outside—in the clouds. You might expect that all our training would have prevented such carelessness, particularly the humiliation of "the chair." But, it didn't. That's because all pilots are subject to being distracted.

When two stimuli are competing for a pilot's attention, the stronger of the two will undoubtedly get it. A battle-damaged airplane "in the soup" is a primary suspect for trouble in every pilot's book. Though a pilot is trained to do a continual cross-check of the instruments, the threat of hydraulic or fuel leaks leading to an engine fire or other grave problems may cause him to be temporarily distracted by the intensity of everything happening around him.

This background intensity may be so strong that the needful stimulus could be momentarily blotted out of the mind. Having cross-checked the instruments, a pilot could overlook the necessary corrections if an urgent radio call interrupted his thought processes or an engine fire suddenly lit up a dozen red signal lights on the warning panel before him. In such a case, even though the instruments were being properly interpreted, vital corrections would be ignored simply because too much was going on.

Only the most experienced man could simultaneously put out an engine fire, make the necessary radio calls, and adjust his descent through the clouds—and then, only with the help of a minor miracle. So, to overcome the intensity of the environment, the ongoing execution of the necessary input was a crucial consideration. Though the cross-check needed to be brief, particularly in an emergency, it needed to be often enough in order to have an impact on the mind, and hence the flying reflexes. All this assumed, of course, that the pilot was still functioning normally.

Temporary incapacitation of the pilot is another cause of accidents. Due to stress, high G-forces, or fragile health, a pilot can also tend to neglect his instruments. That's why, faced with this emergency, I was asking myself if I was still "up to it." The simplest procedures could be overlooked for no other reason than fatigue. You can only push men and machines so far before they begin to crumble, and we had already seen a few planes get beyond repair—and a few pilots.

But strangely enough, in that same vein, there was also the other extreme: the monotony of daily routine. Monotony had the potential for causing several procedural errors. Just as dangerous as the war we were facing were the ten- to fourteen-hour routine hops across the Pacific with their heavy reliance upon the auto-pilot.

The mind needs stimulus. If none is to be found in the routine of life, it will create its own. Constant repetition of the same sensory input will either dull the mind or drive it to distraction. Our instructor went on to tell his wide-eyed audience yet more stories of gear-up landings, taxiing accidents, missed rendezvous points, and the like. These mishaps occurred because men had been lulled into a dulled sense of just functioning. Their vital attentiveness gone, they were just going through the motions instead of staying on the cutting edge of competence. Their spirits were stifled by nothing more stressful than the monotony of the job. Routine.

That day, at the end of the lesson, he concluded, "Remember, gentlemen, normal human functioning is error prone and absent-minded. Consciousness is not continuous." Though at that point we were still a little too young and self-confident to grasp all the implications of his statement, as we matured, we discovered that we were capable of tragic mistakes. Our senses had thresholds above and below which they simply could not operate. As time went on, some of my friends were lost—simply because they were human.

Much of this is true in our spiritual life as well. Christ told His disciples that the spirit is willing but the flesh is weak. We can stay vigilant and absorb only so much because our senses are limited. Faced with distractions, varying degrees of background intensity, fragile health, physical extremes, or prolonged routine, we may find ourselves reacting to life based on nothing more than our last, and somewhat dated, perception of reality. Our last check of the instruments. The "good old days." The way it used to be. Due to the prejudices of that perception, even given the right data, we may unconsciously choose the wrong course of action. Having done so, will it be caught in time?

For a pilot, the margin of error is so fine that one wrong choice can very quickly lead to another. In some cases, a phenomenon known as pilot-induced oscillation can occur, when the pilot's efforts to regain control of the aircraft only aggravate the situation. As it was with that beginning student in "the chair," even a skilled pilot can wind up chasing his wrong first instinct all over the sky if he forgets the disciplines and follows his feelings. And so it goes. Either through the instruments or a disaster, the control problem will be resolved. That is what I was facing in that emergency so long ago. I was alone in the clouds with two realities—and a choice.

"Da Nang Control, this is Nail. Speak to me. I'm in the soup."

And they did. A voice traveled through the medium of the invisible to give me vectors through the clouds. Their navigational beacons grabbed my instruments and pointed them to the runway. To safety. And so it went. Routine.

However, while I was in the clouds, my feelings tried to tell me that the instruments were lying. I had no visible cues outside the cockpit except the occasional false horizon created by the interface of several cloud banks. The minutest changes in energy during acceleration, deceleration, or turns seemed to send the fluids in my inner ear in a whirl. That feedback was telling me that the plane was out of control and the situation desperate. But the instruments kept saying, "No! Don't believe it!"

So I didn't. When the wheels touched down, my head finally stopped spinning as the familiar visible cues became apparent through the ground fog and rain, erasing all doubt. We were down. Safe. The instruments hadn't lied. However, all of my training had certainly been put to the test.

The desert

In another sense, however, so it had been for Christ. "Jesus, full of the Holy Spirit, returned from the Jordan and was led by the Spirit in the desert, where for forty days he was tempted by the devil" (Luke 4:1-2). Jesus had been led into the desert by the same Spirit who had just descended upon Him in the form of a dove. According to the recorded testimony, the heavens opened and a voice clearly said, "You are my Son, whom I love; with you I am well pleased" (Luke 3:22).

Then—*why?*

The question was back. If God the Father loved Him so much and was so pleased with Him . . . why? Why the desert? Why the suffering and pain, only to be faced with the pitiless attack of the enemy? And so I wondered as I finally found time to reflect at the end of that long day.

Having landed safely, it was clear that we would have to remain overnight while the maintenance crews worked the long hours necessary to repair our airplane and get us back into the fray. After debriefing, a lukewarm meal, and coffee at a field kitchen—and a cold shower—we reluctantly climbed back into our sweat-stained clothes. As tired as we were, we were still too wired to go to sleep. Too much had happened. So I walked around the periphery of the base. Concertina wire and revetments now stood between us and an uncertain future. The enemy.

Though I had probably flown over the advance armored columns of the approaching enemy, that same storm that had been so threatening to me had also served to shield me from their guns. As I talked to the guards manning the peripheral outposts of the base, I learned that they weren't expecting anything that night, but, "With Charlie," they said, "you never know! He has a way of hitting you when you least expect it." I continued to walk and pray, and tried to get a grip on myself—and God.

Finally finding a quiet spot, I pulled out my New Testament, and through my imagination I could almost see Jesus as He walked into that desert—and the test. I saw Him tired, hungry, and dirty. Human. As divine as He was, He had felt the obligation to follow the example of Abraham and Moses, so He went into the desert to encounter His Father. Though He had always known God, His mission now was to know Him in a different way, as only a man can: by faith. No supernatural displays of His own power. No special treatment. Just another man—and His faith.

I saw His parched, chapped lips and His body, ema-ciated from His severe fast. Though He had had enough water to survive, He hadn't bathed. His hair was matted to His head. His sweat-stained clothes stuck to His body in the heat of the day, and left Him shivering in the cool of the desert night.

But those stars! The creation! The glory of God and the significance of man, the only creature who could fully appre-ciate his Creator. And talk with Him. Bond to Him. What a sublime experience! But just as Jesus was coming to the end of His strength, another voice spoke—a strange seductive voice. Now, finally, God Himself would experience how all of mankind felt. What it was like to have one's eyes opened to his potential and then have the circumstances of life mutate that living hope into living death.

"If You're the Son of God," the voice said, cynically implying otherwise, "turn this stone into bread." The impli-cation was clear. "Why are You out here starving? Where's Your Father? Didn't He just say that He was pleased with You? So, why didn't He meet Your needs in this wilderness? You'd better take the situation into Your own hands or You'll die, and Your mission will die with You! You're alone out here. Nobody cares! Face it!"

And he was right . . . or so it seemed. Those stars were so far away. And a man, even this man, was so very small. The feelings were not lining up with the promises—and the potential. The facts seemed to be to the contrary. Weakened by hunger, humiliated by ordeal. The enemy knew that now was the moment to strike. The struggle was on. Which reality would Christ choose? The insinuating arguments of His flesh . . . or the promises of God and the call to obedience?

But Christ struck back! "It is written: 'Man does not live

on bread alone.'" And in that response I saw that in spite of the war, we were not just another species of animal driven by instinct. I recognized that man still maintained the potential to rise above his passions of the moment to reach for his God-given potential. In so doing, he could also rise above his circumstances, and maybe even change them. This is the essence of his dignity.

"Oh! It's dignity You want," the voice said. "I can give You that as well. Come along." And so he showed Jesus all the kingdoms of the world with their magnificence. He offered Him power and possessions beyond the wildest dreams of mere men, and, what's more, the earthly means to accomplish His divine ends. If! If He would only forget the promises and live as though God were not there, as if He, the Son of God, were alone in the universe and, hence, left to His own devices.

I saw His struggle . . . and mine. If God was not there, then it was only the smart thing to do to opt for the power. The stuff! If we're really alone down here, then there is only yourself to think about. Be a realist! Everybody else is.

But God had already clearly spoken through the revelation of His creation, the conscience of men, and men of conscience. Even Jesus had to learn the price of integrity— how much it costs to follow the instruments. Correctly interpreting them, He could not be bought. "No," He replied, "you must worship God with all your being . . . and Him only."

"So be it," said the voice. And then, since Jesus spoke of worship, Satan took Him at His word. He wasn't finished yet. The test would go on . . . this time in the Temple. There he challenged Christ to prove that He was not alone. For if God was really there, Satan reasoned, Christ could prove it by putting His precious promises to the test. And he quoted a few. Satan used God's Word to try to seduce His Son. It was a subtle and strong temptation. His purpose was clear. Just as he did in that garden so long ago, he tempted Christ to be more than a mere mortal. By launching His ministry with a publicity stunt, He could surely recruit the masses. By defying the laws of gravity and actually flying—with the help of angels, of course—He could be more than a man! "You will be like God!" (Genesis 3:5). This, perhaps, is the greatest of the temptations. It's certainly the oldest.

But, as obvious as this temptation is, many people lose their faith by insisting that God do something to make life conform to their exaggerated expectations, based on their flawed world view. Often religious people quote Scripture that seems to back up the demand they are making. However, unconsciously they are insisting that some act or gesture or "blessing" is the only possible way God can prove either His presence or His love. So, in throwing themselves from this pinnacle of presumption, they unwittingly respond to the satanic voice by compelling God, pushing the limits of what He made them to be.

As time passes, in their insistence and their impatience their faith is eroded away as they continue to expect from God what He never intended them to experience. Eventually they deny God because He would not conform to their expectations. In joining the ranks of the "realists," there is nothing left then but to take matters into their own hands and follow their own world view. For them, God is no longer there. They're alone in the universe. And now they have proof. Or so they think.

This is why the enemy's attack is so devastating. Once our eyes have left the instruments, the false horizons of the clouds of human opinion will be manipulated by the enemy in such a way that they will interface to form another plausible, believable horizon. With time, our feelings will converge upon this other reality, seducing our senses and eventually substantiating it. The strength of the lie is that it can be proven to be true through observation and experience. For, left to our limited senses only, we are no match for the liar. We will eventually come to the conclusion that God isn't there. We are alone.

But Christ said, "It is also written: 'Do not put the Lord your God to the test.'" For God is God! As I read that, my eyes were opened again to how much more I just had to wait—wait for God. I focused once again on the promise that they who wait upon the Lord shall renew their strength and "they will soar on wings like eagles" (Isaiah 40:31). My concept of myself, my country, and our contribution to humanity were radically changing and I did not want to be numbered among those who forget that God has His own agenda and timetable. I didn't want to listen to that subtle and selfish voice that would insist that God perform a miracle. For its disappointed victims begin the death-spiral characteristic of a pilot who has lost sight of his instruments . . . and the true horizon.

Though I couldn't know it then, unfortunately I would soon learn of that spiral first hand. For now that the plane was repaired and we were somewhat rested, we were back in the fight. We had to stop them!

As I lined up on the runway awaiting my takeoff clearance, I prayed. For, I knew that I was *not* alone.

CHAPTER ELEVEN
A Cry of Faith

Then I heard a loud voice in heaven say:
"Now have come the salvation and the power and
the kingdom of our God, and the authority of his
Christ. For the accuser of our brothers [Satan], who
accuses them before our God day and night, has
been hurled down. They overcame him by the
blood of the Lamb. . . ."
(Revelation 12:10-11)

■

As intense as it had been, it became even more so. Da Nang was now being periodically harassed by 122mm Soviet-made rockets. It was psychological warfare, the enemy's way of sapping our strength and our resolve. We were faced with the threat of a major attack. Everyone was on constant alert. Encumbered with flak jackets and automatic weapons, we continued our duties. Air operations went on. As long as the runway stayed open, we'd go for it. There were just too many people counting on us.

We had to stop them!

In this electrified atmosphere, I performed a rapid pre-flight taxi and takeoff. Now in the air, I felt more at ease. Here I was in command of myself, the plane, a sector, and the other aircraft and pilots assigned to me. Our mission was to destroy the enemy supply lines. Back there on the ground, I had waited in a bunker for what seemed like an eternity for the repairs to be completed. There was little more to do than to seek out the latest intelligence reports and get some rest. I knew my time would come soon enough . . . and it did.

"Nail, this is Olds. How copy?"

A flight of fighters in a loose two-ship combat formation checked in on the preassigned combat frequency. We were all trying to "sterilize" parts of the DMZ in the continued effort to rescue our buddies. Some of them had been down there since the outbreak of the offensive and we still couldn't get to them. It was just too hot. But we had to keep trying!

"Got a target for you, Olds flight," I said, knowing that we'd be up against some stiff resistance.

"Roger," an experienced voice responded. "We're ready to go to work."

"Altimeter: 29.98. Terrain: 20 meters. Come in from New York to Miami. One pass. Expect triple-A," I said matter of factly. We'd resorted to the "New York to Miami" parlance because we knew that Charlie was monitoring the combat frequencies in order to tell their gunners where to look for the kill. By calling for a bomb run from New York to Miami, a southerly heading, we were betting our lives that those listening wouldn't be quick enough to look north of the target and position their guns accordingly. One pass, perhaps, fifteen seconds, was all I felt the traffic could safely bear, given the intensity of the "triple-A" we could expect.

I rolled in, armed my rockets, and laid down a barrage that ignited the jungle around the heavy gun emplacement that had been mercilessly firing on rescue forces for days. While pulling out, I banked to the left to get a better look at the smoke-obscured target, while the fighters about me positioned themselves to roll in as soon as I gave them the clearance. Satisfied with the first run, I gave the orders that I had given a hundred times before. "You're cleared hot. . . .

Hit the smoke!" All we needed were just a few seconds. Just a few seconds more and we could go home. Just one run . . .

The lead aircraft rolled in, his wing man staying high to cover him. As "lead" stabilized the dive for those few seconds necessary to concentrate on his target, what came up at him looked like the spray of a firehose filled with red-hot lead. The rounds glowed in the twilight sky as they sailed past his cockpit, wings, and fuselage at supersonic speed, missing him by just a few yards. He timed his release and a string of five or six bombs disappeared into the dense foliage below.

A second later, the jungle erupted in a red-hot, smoke-filled fireball, as the shock waves of the blast silenced the gun. I rolled inverted and looked carefully at the situation to see if another run was warranted. However, while lead began pulling out of his dive, he caught the last rounds the enemy gun had fired just before his bombs hit. He was unable to avoid the dense, dark wall of exploding antiaircraft fire that surrounded him. The deadly shrapnel riddled his plane. A telltale trail of grey-white smoke behind his aircraft immediately impelled me deeper into rescue operations and emergency procedures.

"Mayday! Mayday! Olds lead, you've taken a hit! You're on fire!"

There was no answer.

"Two," I said, addressing his wing-man, "you got him in sight?"

"Roger."

"See any chutes?"

"No chutes in sight."

"Olds lead," I said, "it looks bad . . . You're trailing smoke." But, there was still no answer. So I shouted, "Lead, you're in trouble . . . Get out! Bail out! Lead . . . do you read me? Lead . . . lead . . . Olds lead, come in . . . How copy?"

Deaf and dumb, the plane a mile off my wing began its

macabre spiral into the jungle floor below. Pilots refer to it as "augering in." The term came from the carpenter's tool, which resembles a large corkscrew, used for boring into wood. It became part of the pilot's jargon because the descending spiral pattern of the tool's razor-sharp thread eerily resembles the flight path of a plane caught in a long, slow, gradual spin. Though a spiral gives the appearance of being under control, in reality it's not. For some reason, the vital interpretation of the instruments breaks down, and unless the crew is shocked back into corrective action, that spiral leads to death.

I called again, "Olds, do you read me? How copy?"

The silence that followed seemed to push reality into the surrealistic, as time and the war stood still. Once again, I was powerless. Though wanting to do so much more, all I could do was watch in the hope of seeing the parachute that would trigger yet another set of trained responses in me. But there was none. Clearly on fire, the plane continued to climb out in a right-hand turn. Then, as though they were flying in slow motion, gradually that climbing turn lost its initial impetus and the nose began to sink heavily into the horizon. Again and again I cried out to them, "Bail out! Bail out!" But still no one answered—still no chutes.

As they hung lifelessly in the sky, I knew the war had condemned me to see it through to its tragic end. Duty. "If only . . . ! Oh, God! If only . . . !" All we had needed was a few seconds. Just a few. But now, as the nose of their crippled plane fell below the horizon, the long, slow descent to death crystallized. With the smoke still trailing behind them, their precious altitude was squandered with each spiral turn. Lower, lower, and lower they went until, through my tears, I screamed into the radios for the last time in the desperate hope of waking one of the two pilots, apparently knocked unconscious by those fatal rounds of gunfire. But it was to no avail. There was just silence, smoke, and a spiral whose tightening turns bored through what little altitude was left . . . and they augered in.

The death spiral

Since then, I've seen other spirals and, at times, have been caught in them myself. Though they were of a spiritual nature, they were just as deadly. For the believer, they begin when our eyes leave the instruments and we unconsciously start to demand from God what He never intended us to have. Or, we begin looking to get out of life what it was never designed by its Creator to deliver. In doing so, we blunder into that faith-killing insistence that God answer up to our world view. In doing so, our demands resemble that satanic temptation to leap from the pinnacle of the Temple. In reality, it may have no greater spiritual purpose in our lives than to force God to prove He is there . . . to our satisfaction. Caught in the height of presumption, we insist that the Creator serve the creature. When He doesn't, we "take a hit," and the spiral begins.

Disillusionment—As it progresses, we find ourselves disappointed, stunned, disillusioned. But when we are feeling disillusioned, it's because we've been under the influence of an illusion that, like a mirage in the desert, vanishes under closer scrutiny. In our insistence, however, we tell ourselves that if we invest more time, effort, money, and energy, our desire is more likely to come to pass. And so man has been sacrificing since the beginning—for his world view. But what of God's eternal agenda?

Disappointment and disillusionment are the first warning signals telling us that our eyes have momentarily strayed from the instruments and our unconscious desires have subtly moved beyond what God has intended for us at the moment. The essence of sin is overreaching, that is, placing expectations on life that are beyond God's parameters.

We face an enemy who wants to keep us from pulling out of the death spiral once it has begun. His primary tactic is to keep us from getting back on the instruments and his primary weapon is accusation. He's known as an accuser who accuses us daily before God and man. Like an enemy gunner, he fires his salvos of guilt, incessantly prodding us toward self-criticism. He's an expert at tearing people apart. He makes sure that we see the flaws in our own character and certainly in the character of others.

In getting our focus off God's love, Satan can twist the sense of Scripture itself in order to seemingly prove that our faith was ill-founded. Where the Bible speaks of love, he will point out, as he did with Christ in the desert, how much love we have *not* received. Where Scripture speaks of justice, he will clearly point out the justice we have *not* received. And so on. He will accuse, accuse, and accuse again. Finally, as we find ourselves pushed into his camp, we will begin to agree with him. As we do so, the spiral tightens.

Discouragement—To lose heart or one's courage is the essence of discouragement. And though we all get to that point time and again—particularly when it comes to the people and projects that have meant the most to us—we must recognize that the spiral is now in a more aggravated state. We've fallen deeper into the merciless hands of the accuser. For if we continue to listen to the accusations—all that is wrong, all that is missing, all that is *not* happening the way we would like it to—eventually we will begin to find reasons for feeling that life itself is against us. Alone. But coming to that conclusion, though apparently justifiable, does not resolve the problem of what is *not* happening, either in our lives or in the lives of those around us. In our "aloneness," as the frustration and guilt feelings mount, we discover that we are also answerless.

Depression—Feeling alone and estranged from life often leads to depression. When we fail to find an answer or a world view strong enough to deal with the discouragement of this life, the spiral continues. Faced with a growing awareness of all that is missing, or at least appears to be missing, we spin downward into depression. Depending on how far into it we have gone, we experience either listlessness and a general lack of enthusiasm for life or a pronounced, stoic silence and withdrawal from those we love. Finally, there are the more acute cases when a person is no longer able to function in a normal manner and needs to be hospitalized.

Much of the post-traumatic syndrome, "combat fatigue," that a minority of Vietnam veterans have experienced is an advanced state of depression. Having faced a murderous reality that was too brutal, too discouraging for their youthful idealism, these men needed years to give the heart and mind enough time to digest what they faced over there. If you have ever skirted the edge of depression, as I have, you know that trying to put it all back together and coming to some coherent explanation about the meaning of life, or at least your own life, is a difficult task. Picking up the pieces of life's broken puzzle, even if you still have the energy of youth, is never easy. But time can heal, if we are listening to the right voice. Failure to get the right kind of help, however, will surely lead to the final phase of the spiritual death spiral.

Despair—It is at this point that the accuser demonstrates his greatest genius and subtlety. He offers despair—as a form of hope! That is, the pain of trying to figure it all out is so great that he helps us come to the seemingly logical and rational explanation that we are alone in the universe. So, there is nothing to figure out! It's all absurd. The pain and suffering have no real meaning, and so we should stop looking for it. Ceasing to look for a greater, transcendent truth, according to the accuser, helps us "cope" with present realities. Accepting this bitter truth, he says, frees us up to take care of ourselves. We are no longer naive children looking for God. We're realists. Living in despair saves us from any disappointments in the future. We're free to expect nothing more from life. And, unfortunately, that's what we get: nothing!

This somewhat nihilistic world view, which is too often the logical consequence of great pain and disappointment, may actually help us move out of depression and, in a grim way, get on with life. However, the mind tends to become forever closed to the idea of a personal God who cares and, hence, a higher purpose for mankind. With time, we then move from despair into the kind of cynicism that masquerades as realism. With more time, we may even become evangelists of despair, openly mocking those who are still looking for an ennobling purpose to it all.

The image comes back to mind of that older veteran shouting down the younger one's questioning: "Shut up and sit down, Socrates! Welcome to the world!" Those words were neither realistic nor wise. They represented the pathetic and answerless cry of despair, the voice of one who had missed his encounter with the Divine and had surrendered to the arguments of the accuser. It was clear to all who knew him. Like so many, the turns of that veteran's spiritual spiral bore deeper and deeper into the icy indifference of the age . . . and he augered in.

The cry of faith

Returning from that mission, I was under the incessant attack of the accuser. Why didn't I foresee the possibility? But, I had! Why didn't I call his run in from a safer direction? But, I had! I picked the direction after studying the terrain with binoculars—and dodging some of the same flak to do so. Why didn't I clear him sooner—or later? But, the timing was right! And so my inner dialogue went. And I was losing. The day before it had been the chopper. Now . . .

The other days—the happier days, the successful rescues, the days when the guns had been silenced without a loss—paled into the distant background when compared with this day's pain and self-doubt. The chopper . . . now, this. And the offensive showed no signs of letting up. Would we stop them? Could we? I began to think the unthinkable. But, as real as those questions were for us all, my mind was focused on something much smaller than the war, but far more important to my personal future: my role in it all.

Had I been negligent with respect to that crew? Could I have done it better? Had my conscience been as sensitive to my professional training as it needed to be at that moment? What about the other moments, the other days? Days when I had to "prune" a gun on the edge of a village. Days when I had to hit a staging area, knowing that it might also very well be a field hospital. Days of trying to save a village that was being overrun, knowing that I couldn't control where every ricocheted bullet went. And in it all, there were always the innocent, the women and children. There were the days when we would make all the right decisions, only to see the hazards of war negate them. What about all that?

The accuser was relentless . . . pitiless . . . merciless. It was almost as though I heard his audible, laughing voice sneering at me, "And you call yourself a Christian?" Like Paul, I knew what the law and conscience said. Like Paul, I realized that given the situation, I wouldn't be able to obey the law and the voice of my conscience—without help. Like Paul, I cried out, "Who will rescue me from this body of death?" Where could I go . . . to whom could I go . . . with all this?

In Alexander Solzhenitsyn's apocalyptic vision of the future, *From Under the Rubble*, the past stands out as a mirror of what the future might hold if man does not turn back from his self-destructive willfulness. Describing in painful detail what it was like for Russia to lose twenty million people during the last war, he talked about the treason, betrayal, and despair that seized his people during those dark days when Stalin ruled with an iron fist. Surrounded by death, destruction, and the deep wounds of great loss, coming out from under the rubble became as much a psychological struggle as it was a profound physical necessity. Why do it? For whom? For what? In essence, his people were paralyzed by the past. They couldn't forget; they couldn't forgive. The wounds were too deep. Despair reigned, and justifiably so.

Then, Solzhenitsyn went on to ask the compelling questions: Where could they take such pain, sorrow, and disappointment? Where could they leave it? What event was big enough to give Russia and all of humanity a fresh start after such barbarity? Who was big enough to silence the accuser when so much of what he was saying was so justifiable? So much was *not* right with the world! With *life*! Who, finally, could take so many scarred people and lift them out of their inevitable despair?

There was only one, he said, who could lead us to the forgiveness of ourselves, others—and a new life. The Christ! And only one event in history could have so profoundly marked it that, in spite of the accuser, man could still face life with hope. God died to redeem history! The blood of the Lamb overcomes the accuser by taking all the guilt and shame and, from God's perspective, washing it away. And it can do the same from our perspective as well, *if* we will only let it.

Against the backdrop of despair, the need for salvation, even for a religious man like Paul, becomes evident. Caught in the conscious awareness of his inability to obey the law, Paul knew how much he was missing the mark. He knew only too well how devastating the accuser could be. He was aware of what he was not doing that he *should* do, and of what he was doing that he should *not* do. In the hands of the accuser, the law had become a bludgeon that condemned Paul, pushing him to the brink of despair—something I, too, had experienced.

But that fateful day, as I read again of Paul's struggle, my heart seized the significance of his victorious cry: the cry of faith. "There is now no condemnation for those who are in Christ Jesus, because through Christ Jesus the law of the Spirit of life set me free from the law of sin and death" (Romans 8:1-2).

At the Cross, God offered man the power to silence the accuser and pull out of the spiral. A new principle was set in motion by which the moral order of the universe would now be governed. No condemnation!! God's ultimate intention was clearly revealed, in spite of what the accuser and his cynical adepts say. God wants a *relationship*! How, then, could we be alone? Ever since the Cross, that relationship is now possible if we will live according to that new life-giving principle that sets us free from the spiral . . . and death.

CHAPTER TWELVE
The Counselor

*If the Spirit of him who raised Jesus from the dead
is living in you, he who raised Christ from the dead
will also give life to your mortal bodies through his
Spirit, who lives in you.*
(Romans 8:11)

■

That day, I couldn't breathe my characteristic sigh of relief as I walked away from the airplane, even though I was one more mission closer to the freedom flight. Somewhere out there in the still burning jungle were the charred remains and twisted metal of what was once a manned weapons system. I had had my fill of war for the day—and perhaps for a lifetime. I felt . . . old.

Death had once again gouged out the idealism of youth and gripped me in its downward spiral. Though I continued to function, primarily by reflex, I realized that if God Himself did not enter into the picture—if I did not experience God's love and forgiveness, in spite of all that had transpired, just as Paul had done—then I, too, would eventually "auger in." The accuser's condemnation was overwhelming. And the battle dragged on. Not only was I fighting for a few downed comrades helplessly trying to evade the enemy in the jungle, but now, more than ever, my own soul seemed to be hanging in the balance.

Having gone through the ordeal of reporting the loss of the crew to the people at Intell, and having answered yet again the questions that seemed so meaningless in comparison to my higher quest for meaning, I plopped down in my hammock and tried to think of other days. Happier days when life was younger, sweeter, far away from death and failure. Days when, on the threshold of manhood, it seemed possible to right the world, slay all the dragons, and remain untarnished in the process. Days when I enjoyed family and friends, the Academy, and the subsequent year of pilot training.

Even the shocking experience of that first spin now had a certain appeal. What would I have done that day without the instructor pilot? He had seen it all before, flying through the recovery procedure time and time again. Yet he patiently worked with me, even though the circumstances had literally made me sick in his presence. He answered my questions and calmed my fears. In the final analysis, he believed in me. He already knew what I didn't: that I could *do* it. His quiet but firm presence not only made it possible for me to pull out of a spin, a death spiral, but gave me the confidence necessary to face it again and again.

I was not alone.

But now, just two years later, who could I turn to? I was calling the shots. I had the responsibility for the missions. Though in this respect the situation was different, in many ways the basic need was still the same. Who could help me face it all? Though outwardly we all functioned as we had been trained to do, inwardly there were the same unresolved questions. Could I do it? Would I make it? As I plunged into my Bible, I realized just how personal the ministry of the Holy Spirit could be.

I was not alone!

That day, as that spiritual death spiral subtlely set in, I had been tempted to look again to my own resources, my own limited world view, to find the answers. Something. Anything! After all, my own resources had seemed to work in those happier, easier days, which were now so very distant. But, faced with all this . . . !

As the spiral progressed, I began to feel discouraged, even guilty. The spiritual enemy, with his insinuations and outright accusations, heightened my awareness of what was wrong with this war until I could no longer see it objectively.

I did not want to psychologically "eject" as many had already done. Feeling abandoned, they disengaged from the pursuit of any meaning at all. Sullen, bordering on despair, they seemed to be augering in. Yet in my heart I knew that God had never intended a death spiral for man. Faced with my own death spiral, I prayed. In my heart, in the privacy of my corner of the Quonset hut, I acknowledged my need for God. The spiral was broken. I began to "pull out" only when I finally admitted I could not do it on my own. But in doing so, I made a startling discovery.

I was not alone . . . "because those who are led by the Spirit of God are sons of God. For you did not receive a spirit that makes you a slave again to fear, but you received the Spirit of sonship. And by him we cry, 'Abba, Father.' The Spirit himself testifies with our spirit that we are God's children" (Romans 8:14-16).

From a slave to a son!
The animism of the Orient is based on the assumption that there is a spirit world to be appeased. That is, if a person, anyone, is not careful, his "luck" will change if he angers one of the unseen ancestral beings that surround him continually. Most religions, including certain incomplete aspects of Christianity, share this superstition. According to this way

of thinking, there is a vengeful God, gods, or spirits who cannot be appeased or placated unless people submit themselves in slavery to the practice of rituals and sacrifices. Almost without exception, this fear is the motor of the world's religions: the fear of being condemned by someone or something that can't be seen or known.

Given this backdrop, a believer—who has the Holy Spirit of love—is the essence of freedom itself. Even in the Judaism of Paul's day, most "religious" people lived in mortal fear of judgment. As holy as the law was, it had become a whip in the hands of the accuser and his unwitting henchmen. It spoke of punishment for those who failed to follow it. Its god, the god of law, was beyond the reach of mere mortals. Only the selected few would even think of entering his presence. Having done so, they might dare to speak of love, but always on the backdrop of fear. Condemnation.

This was the essential nature of my struggle, as well. I feared God, in the sense that I respected Him. But I now also knew what was not right with myself and my world. Having lived for eighteen months in a war zone that appeared to be increasingly Godforsaken with every day, I struggled with my seemingly meager spiritual armaments just to keep some semblance of a coherent faith—and some grounds for youthful optimism.

But, we were just too far from WW II and Korea. The world had changed and so had we. I was just one of many young officers who realized that our lives were little more than cogs in a great war machine that had gotten bogged down in the incomprehensible forces of history, politics, and culture. The human condition. Outside of the personal integrity and courage of the individual combatants, there was little to illuminate the darkness that surrounded me—except God. His Spirit was faithfully giving testimony to my spirit that I belonged to Him. "Abba, Father!" I was not alone.

A Counselor

This is why Christ's teachings were so revolutionary, and why, throughout history, they have continued to liberate all who would dare to follow them. For, when Christ promised His disciples that His physical presence among them would be replaced by the spiritual reality of the Comforter, they, like myself, didn't seem to grasp the significance of it all. God in the flesh, performing miracles and teaching, seemed much more preferable to the twelve than some ethereal yet-to-be-proven presence of God in the individual life. However, I was astounded, as I'm sure they were, when I began to reflect upon Christ's promise to us all: "I will ask the Father, and he will give you another Counselor to be with you forever—the Spirit of truth. The world cannot accept him, because it neither sees him nor knows him. But you know him, for he lives with you and will be in you. . . . All this I have spoken while still with you. But the Counselor, the Holy Spirit, whom the Father will send in my name, will teach you all things and will remind you of everything I have said to you" (John 14:16-17, 25-26).

The word "counselor" means an advocate or helper of anyone who has run afoul of the law. In the courtroom of life, He comes to our rescue as we face a determined prosecutor who accuses us "before our Father day and night" (Revelation 12:10). This accuser would always have us believe that our hardships are the "proof" that God does not love us and that our lives are out of control. He's relentless. But the Counselor speaks to these same struggles, giving "testimony" to the truth that our relationship to God was radically changed at the Cross. "It is God who justifies. Who is he that condemns? Christ Jesus, who died—more than that, who was raised to life—is at the right hand of God and is also interceding for us" (Romans 8:33-34).

In spite of the real difficulties and even the tragedies of

this life, we can live as a forgiven people. Pardoned! New hope, new horizons! And as severely as the accuser condemns, so much more powerful will the ministry of the Spirit be, teaching us and reminding us of all that Christ has said and done, and continues to say and do. Though the prosecutor "fires away" constantly, exposing all our sins of commission and omission, we can nevertheless hear the pardon of the righteous Judge of the universe, who loves us where we are, as we are. "There is now no condemnation for those who are in Christ Jesus . . ." (Romans 8:1). And thus the enemy's guns are silenced!

However, while I was discovering this, guns of another kind, which still surrounded our downed comrades in the jungle, continued their murderous fire and inflicted a heavy toll on men, machines, and morale. The realization that I did not have to fear the condemnation of God changed everything—and yet it changed nothing. Inside me, there was a glimmer of hope. I felt freed of the incessant accusations and the downward spiral they tried to produce. But outside, there was still the problem of pain. A war. And an enemy offensive with determination that had rarely been equaled in this war or any other.

I found myself routinely going through the motions of getting ready to face it all again. There was no way I could relive the last few days and bring the helicopter crew or the two pilots in that fighter back to life. I somehow had to get all that behind me. Praying had definitely helped, but I needed more time, a luxury I just didn't have.

We had to stop them!

In the ready room it was all the same. The map was the same, though the position markers had changed. The briefing was the same, though the briefing officer had changed. Then, we were joined by the "old man." Apparently, this mission was going to be a little different. But, then again, not really. Someone had finally installed a new air conditioner, but with the rising temperatures and tempers, it hardly seemed to matter. With the briefing completed, I rode the same personnel carrier out to the same parked aircraft, surrounded by the same maintenance crews, loading the same fuel and ordnance. Nothing had changed—and yet everything had.

I was not alone!

That day, I had one week to go. Soon I would be home. "Back in the world," as we used to say. But now, at age twenty-five, I was one of the most experienced men in the theater. I was a veteran. But, an anxious one. It wasn't my personal safety that concerned me as much as it was what the war might once again call upon me to do. What I would later have to live with!

Completing the same preflight, taxi, and takeoff in the same sweltering heat, I rendezvoused with Navy and Air Force fighters in yet another effort to back the guns off of our men in the hopes of making a rescue. But now heavy anti-aircraft artillery was camouflaged among the numerous villages that dotted the countryside. The reconnaissance had been perfect and the photos at Intell quite clear. In many ways this mission was going to be tough. With the help of computers and laser-guided ordnance, we would have to selectively prune certain dwellings on the edge of a village that were clearly being used as gun emplacements.

Up until now, in spite of our losses, we had been relatively successful in dealing with the guns and maintaining air superiority. But that had been in the jungle. Combatants only. Men who had known the rules of the game and had been prepared to take it to the bitter end if need be. Now the rules were changing. Villages were being overrun, and though the refugees fleeing in front of the invasion forces numbered in the hundred of thousands, we could be sure that there were just as many who hadn't fled their sacred lands, willing to bend with the breeze of the warring factions as they had been doing for generations. Tao.

So, what to do? The murderous presence of the guns was incontestable, but now they would also be surrounded by villagers. And we still had to stop them. Without the lasers, the mission would have been out of the question. But, a handful of us had been trusted with this state-of-the-art technology. At the briefing, the old man himself made sure that we understood the new "ROE" (rules of engagement) in light of the continued advance of the enemy. The situation was precarious enough that this kind of mission would have to be considered. It fell on us.

And so we silenced the guns. Men were rescued. But . . .

Even though the accuracy of the new space-age technology was uncanny in its effectiveness, to this day I still wonder, and I take counsel of the Counselor. Life is difficult. Hard situations bring about hard choices—and pain. Pain for us and those around us. And though I knew I was a child of God, I still had to face life. The difference being, I was not alone. "Endure hardship as discipline; God is treating you as sons. For what son is not disciplined by his father? . . . No discipline seems pleasant at the time, but painful. Later on, however, it produces a harvest of righteousness and peace for those who have been trained by it" (Hebrews 12:7,11).

As much as I wanted it to be otherwise, I was not going to be excused from wrestling with life. I was not going to be given a waiver from the crushing weight of adult responsibility and decision making. Though everything was different, everything would be the same. I was not going to be able to avoid the hardships of a world living "east of Eden." Not only did I need the assurance that God could look upon my life with compassion in the midst of it all, but I also needed to know that there would be active concern, involvement. I wanted to assume the responsibilities of a son. But after all I had experienced, I needed help sorting out what that meant—what was worthy, authentic, and true.

A guide

Being freed from the slavery of the guilt and fear that motivates religion without love, I could look to the future knowing that in spite of my painful past, God was for me (Romans 8:31). New beginnings were possible, but not without training or discipline. I knew that God had a project in mind for mankind—and for a man. Righteousness. Surrounded as I was by the accuser's "proof" that God did not care, I was assured by Christ's promise that I was not alone. "I have much more to say to you, more than you can now bear. But when he, the Spirit of truth, comes, he will guide you into all truth. . . . The Spirit will take from what is mine and make it known to you" (John 16:12-15).

Truth can be a very bitter pill to swallow if we are not ready for it. As with that introductory flight I took years before, there is a big difference between wanting to fly and being able to handle a spin. Encounters with the truth, whether it be about God, life, or—the hardest to deal with—ourselves, can lead to profound confusion and a sense of being overwhelmed. A spin! That spin can become a death spiral if we listen to the wrong voice and refuse the discipline and training of the Instructor. As rough as that may seem to be at times, it's guidance.

Christ promised that the truth would set us free (John 8:32). First and foremost, we're free from guilt and fear. But as we relate to God in love, He continues to free us from the lies and half-truths that surround us. Stripping us of ego, illusion, and the unnecessary baggage created by our pride, God's truth will put our feet on the firm ground upon which we can build—or rebuild—a life, a family, and, ultimately, a country. All this truth will be effective for us *if*, in the humiliation of the learning process, we'll put our confidence in God.

We're not alone!

As the helicopters carried some of my rescued buddies back to base that day, I felt buoyed. Apparently, the enemy's orders had changed. We'd finally broken the back of their offensive. But, it had forced us to take risks, and to consider even the unthinkable when it came to mission strategy. Stress, weariness, and fear, the routine of our existence at those remote bases, had caused us to come up with relative ethics, relative "truths" by which we tried to live with and control a war. A "truth" that had left us no option . . . we had to stop them!

As I lived in the middle of such relativistic ethics, I learned that we can only partially escape the influence of our environment. Our ethics are always relative, and our so-called truths are flawed. As Paul said, our world views, even as Christians, are woefully incomplete. "Now we see but a poor reflection as in a mirror; then we shall see face to face. Now I know in part; then I shall know fully, even as I am fully known" (1 Corinthians 13:12).

One day I will know what I should have done and what I should not have done (2 Corinthians 5:10). We all will. One day I will see how God has not abandoned mankind, even though mankind's abandonment of Him led to a world filled with war, racism, disease, famine, and death. One day, I will fully understand and be privy to the very counsel of God Himself. One day, "I shall know. . . ." We all will.

But until then, we can be sure of only one thing: in spite of it all, He loves us. "Who shall separate us from the love of Christ? Shall trouble or hardship or persecution or famine or nakedness or danger or sword? . . . No, in all these things we are more than conquerors through him who loved us. For I am convinced that neither death nor life, neither angels nor demons, neither the present nor the future, nor any powers, neither height nor depth, nor anything else in all creation, will be able to separate us from the love of God that is in Christ Jesus our Lord" (Romans 8:35-39).

We are not alone!

Knowing this, we can wait upon God.

CHAPTER THIRTEEN
Wings of Faith

*The word of God is living and active. Sharper than
any double-edged sword, it penetrates even to
dividing soul and spirit, joints and marrow; it
judges the thoughts and attitudes of the heart.*
(Hebrews 4:12)

∎

It was time to go home. We had broken the back of the
Easter Offensive, bought our allies the time they desperately
needed to regroup, and brought the North Vietnamese back
to the negotiating tables in Paris. Having finally rescued the
last of our downed buddies who had not yet been captured
or killed, we watched and waited as the war reverted back to
that uneasy, deathly calm that had preceded the Easter
storm.

How long it would last, no one knew, but it was clear
that a page in the war's history—and mine—had turned. It
was time to move on. Reeling with the realization that I'd
been "spared"—for what?—I began to unwind. I needed a
rest. Any efficiency I had attained during the last few weeks
was due to adrenaline and coffee . . . and the grace of God. It
was time for the freedom flight. Time to go home.

While packing, I came across my flight manual and

nostalgically leafed through it once more. We were old friends. On its tattered cover was the picture of the airplane I flew: the OV-10 Bronco. In many ways this book had become my second Bible. I had spent literally hundreds of hours studying its now well-worn pages. However, in a few days, I would start the process all over again. Going home to a new assignment and a new type of aircraft, I would receive a new flight manual, whose contents I would once again have to master.

For, not only had that pilot training, years ago, impressed upon us all the absolute necessity of trusting our instruments, but in a shocking way it had made us very serious students of the flight manuals, as well. In one of our introductory lessons, we were shown the now infamous film of an experienced pilot trapped in the death throes of his own ignorance. The opening sequence of the film showed nothing out of the ordinary as he made his final approach to the runway in an experimental aircraft.

The team filming the plane as it landed in various flap configurations and airspeeds was probably getting ready to wind up a routine day when the aircraft started to drop too low on the glide slope. The pilot reacted normally, adding power and pulling up on the nose. However, this film taught all the pilots of that airplane in the years to come that even a "normal" reaction at such a low airspeed, given that flap configuration, could lead to the unexpected—and unfortunate.

The camera faithfully recorded the tragedy for the professionals testing the plane—and for posterity. As the pilot continued to pull up on the nose, the aircraft "stalled" far more radically than anyone would have guessed. Losing altitude, the plane wobbled through the air out of control. As the film went into slow motion, we watched for several seconds as the pilot went into afterburner (full throttle) in order to forestall what was now obvious to everyone. He was not going to make it and he did not have enough airspeed to safely eject. We could only imagine what the pilot's final thoughts were, as we watched the plane mush into the runway out of control, bounce, cartwheel from wing tip to wing tip, and explode. The film ended in flames, smoke . . . and silence. The instructor had our undivided attention.

The manual

"Some of the information contained in your flight manual may very well have cost the life of a test pilot!" the major said in an effort to impress upon us just how important the book was. And he succeeded. From that point on, he went through the manual section by section so that we would not miss anything that could be of value to us on the day we soloed.

Each section contained a thorough discussion of the major design components of the aircraft, such as hydraulics, avionics, engines, and the like. What the engineers felt the pilot needed to know about the aircraft in order to enhance its performance was clearly outlined, giving warnings, cautions, and notes in specific detail. The book spoke not only of the necessary care and maintenance of the parts, but also of the intended performance parameters of the plane itself. This went on for hundreds of pages.

Set aside from the normal operating procedures of start, taxi, takeoff, and recovery were the "red pages"—the emergency procedures! In them, such difficulties as engine flameout, or fire, electronic failures, instrument failure, and control problems were discussed in very specific detail. The engineers and test pilots, having thoroughly hashed out the problems that had arisen or could possibly arise, had come up with checklists to deal with each possible scenario. The items on the checklists were so critical that they had to be memorized and rehearsed in the simulators, over and over again, before a pilot was considered ready to handle the plane safely.

For weeks on end these procedures were reviewed. Nothing could be missed. Too much was at stake. The tedium of the exercise was at times fatiguing and there were moments when it seemed that the instructor would never let up. Frustration would mount as day after day he would spring another emergency on us. "OK! You're in icing conditions and your instruments have started to act erratically. What are you going to do?" Or, "You've just had a flameout, your hydraulic pressure is dropping, and your controls are not responding properly. What are you going to do?" And on and on it went. The man who hesitated too long in giving his response was reprimanded with a curt, "Do you want to fly or don't you, mister?" The truth was brutal. It had to be!

For, if you didn't have it memorized and rehearsed in your mind beforehand, it was certain that under the pressure of the actual emergency, you would not think of it. You'd freeze—or panic! Add to these emergencies the added stress of combat and the complications of possible combat damage and you just couldn't be casual about it. It was not just a matter of completing the mission or just "efficiency." It was a matter of life and death! So, having seen a test pilot drive his airplane into the runway and be swallowed in flames, not a single student pilot in the room that day was ever going to neglect their "second Bible," the manual that revealed the designer's plan. It was unthinkable.

So why does the church ignore its manual?

The Scriptures

Do we intuitively know what the Designer had in mind for life? What were we designed for? Having set the universe in motion in the process of creating life, God brought forth mankind with unique qualities in order to fulfill a certain role or mission in His eternal plan. What is it? Does a casual glance at man and the human condition suffice to tell us, or is it logical to assume that we would need the Designer's input in the learning process? If so, where should we go to get it?

Even though an experienced pilot is usually able to recognize certain design characteristics needed to facilitate the performance of a plane in a given mission, that in itself is far from knowing how to fly it. My first look at the OV-10 was a deceptive one. The engineer had given it a rather conventional design, with two large prop-jet engines under the wing. Even though I could see the racks for the ordnance that would later serve me so well, the plane didn't look at all threatening.

However, my introductory flight showed me just how maneuverable it was and how well-designed it had been to operate within the parameters of its mission: light-strike reconnaissance. As I poured over the flight manual, I discovered how well the project engineers had designed it to function in the unconventional war we were facing in Vietnam. As I made the conscious effort needed to master what its designers had in mind, I was able to clearly visualize what to do and when. The learning process completed, the plane, myself, and the mission became one.

And so it should be for the believer. If God can create a universe, displaying His extraordinary power and incredible attention to detail by bringing forth intelligent life—"in His image"—it seems logical that He would also communicate with those beings. The same Spirit that moved over the primordial chaos to bring about light and order has continued to move throughout the history of man, causing him to reflect on his origins and the meaning of this incredible display known as the creation. Theologians refer to this as the "general revelation" of God to all men.

This to a large extent explains why man is so religious. Something about the vast expanse of the universe is overwhelming, humbling. It is this kind of humility that is essential to the learning process in the spiritual domain. For, through this continued interplay of the creation and man, the Spirit has touched the conscience, whispering. At first, it was to a few—the courageous. But, as these men listened and followed, the whisper became a voice, and they entered into a meaningful dialogue with their Creator. As time went on, their enriching insights became the legacy that claims to speak of the Designer's plan. Something "God-breathed." Theologians refer to this as the "special revelation" of God through His inspired Word and its ultimate Incarnation in the person of Christ. If God can create a universe, logic demands that He can also inspire and protect a manual that is useful in explaining it. "All Scripture is God-breathed and is useful for teaching, rebuking, correcting and training in righteousness, so that the man of God may be thoroughly equipped for every good work" (2 Timothy 3:16-17).

This is what the Bible claims to be. The manual. Having read it, however, does not prevent us from encountering the thunderstorms on our flight path or the flak of the enemy in the spiritual war that surrounds us. However, having studied it, we share the Author's insights into what our performance capabilities should be as we face our enemies and what resources we have at our disposal to overcome them. It's a training manual that helps us through the learning process of life, revealing, correcting, and teaching us about the nature of God, man, and righteousness. It's a very useful book.

Having researched its origins, I've become more and more impressed by the Bible's harmony. Over forty people from various walks of life, from the poorest to the richest, from the weakest to the most powerful, have written over sixty dovetailing treatises on the theme of God and man.

During the period of fifteen hundred years, each author, in his own style and language, told his story and the story of his times in such a way that the unique potential of man as a child of God had to be faced and faced honestly.

Though the parchments have been passed down through the generations, and though heresies, apostasies, and inquisitions have been committed, leaving their tragic marks on human history, there have been countless archaeological discoveries to remind us that the Bible we hold in our hands is what was actually written down so long ago. But the question remains: Will we learn from it? The apostle says, "These things happened to them as examples and were written down as warnings for us, on whom the fulfillment of the ages has come" (1 Corinthians 10:11).

A pilot is not ready to push the aircraft to the limits of its performance envelope until the dangers of going beyond it are so ingrained in him that it becomes unthinkable. Just as the design engineer will issue clear warnings about what to avoid in the way of flight procedures, so God has inspired men to do the same with respect to the way we are designed. God's manual is essential for understanding His love for us and the fulfillment we can find in Him. If we reach for that manual in faith, we, too, might model the greatest of examples, the Christ, who said, "If you hold to my teaching, you are really my disciples. Then you will know the truth, and the truth will set you free" (John 8:31-32).

What is truth?

Strangely enough, in those closing days of my tour of duty in a war zone, as the missions now took off without me, I reflected on the life of yet one more soldier given the thankless job of trying to responsibly handle his country's authority and power in a relatively hostile situation. Though our lives, times, and motivations were different, we did share one basic struggle in common: we'd both been caught between "a truth" and truth.

Pontius Pilate was a pragmatist. Having to face the daily necessity of living with an explosive political situation, he had become, as many of us do, an expert in trying to keep his hands clean and his career intact. Though historians tell us that his assignment to Palestine, a traditional trouble spot in the Roman Empire, was not considered one of the better ones, he handled it well and was probably hoping to forge a reputation for himself back in Rome.

Things were going relatively well until an accused carpenter named Jesus stood before him and presented an alternative to everything he had ever known. This Jesus spoke of a kingdom founded upon the truth. Pilate was troubled. Politics! This man could cause repercussions back in Rome if the turbulent Jewish community was not placated. But, as this rather ordinary looking Messiah went on to say that those who seek the truth hear Him, Pilate retorted with one of the most significant questions recorded in Scripture: "What is truth?" (John 18:38).

Try as he may, Pilate neither understood the silent strength of the man who confronted him nor the turmoil in his own soul. Something told him that this itinerant rabbi was innocent and that the fault lay with Jesus' accusers. But, forces had been set in motion. Though the remnants of his conscience tried to speak out—"I find no basis for a charge against him"—his solitary voice was shouted down by a crowd who wanted a "patriot" named Barabbas. All the water in Jerusalem could not wash that sacred blood from Pilate's hands that day. In order to keep the peace, he crucified its prince. Expediency had had the final say . . . or so it seemed.

As I looked back at my situation after a year in intense combat, I, too, felt that expediency had had the final say. For, any man who has participated in a war knows that truth is its first victim. When blood starts to flow, peoples, tribes, and nations have to come up with reasons to justify it. "A truth." Who is our friend, our foe, right or wrong? And so on. Having decided these things often too hastily, we begin to operate on the basis of expediency, the automatic reaction patterns of a given world view. And so we are all to some extent prisoners of expediency.

Our world view has already dictated who is right or wrong: the conservatives or liberals; the marginals, minorities, or the mainstream; the Democrats or Republicans; our church or theirs. And even more than these social, religious, and political influences, we find ourselves tyrannized by the "bottom line" of personal and corporate finances. And we act accordingly, often joining the conspiracy of silence that refuses to see and hear very clear alternatives. Truth. To the extent that we are caught in these automatic reactions, the true intent of our Designer is blocked.

His Word is truth!

Truth is what sets us free to fulfill the Designer's plan. All else is pretense. And the One who claimed that He was truth incarnate dared to humble the religious leaders of His day by teaching them of a "good Samaritan," a despised person on the margin of respectable society who dared to love in spite of the socioeconomic barriers of his day. Freed from a value system more or less tied to the expedient, he could move toward the essential. Love. This, the apostle says, is the sum total of Scripture. The plan. "You, my brothers, were called to be free. But do not use your freedom to indulge the sinful nature; rather, serve one another in love. The entire law is summed up in a single command: 'Love your neighbor as yourself'" (Galatians 5:13).

As simple as it is to say "love," we are still swept up in

values that force new or twisted definitions of the word upon us, which no longer include its most essential ingredient: the Christ. For, we are to love as He loved: "A new command I give you: Love one another. As I have loved you, so you must love one another" (John 13:34). We were designed to give of ourselves, even to the point of sacrifice, if necessary. To lay down our lives for others, as Jesus did.

However, this kind of love is a function of our basic attitude toward ourselves, God, and the earthly focus of all love: our fellow man. How do we see them? Through the eyes of expediency? Are they the means to some corporate or personal ends awash with passion, power, and the lust to possess? Or, have we broken through to love? Only truth, God's truth, put through the crucible of time and testing, can set us free from the counterfeits of love, which are filled with self-justification and the necessary trappings of expediency.

Truth arose from the tomb to which expediency had consigned it. Truth came back to teach and liberate the disciples from the fear that had scattered them just before the Cross. Truth came back to focus and concentrate them, to "sanctify" them, in light of the Designer's plan. And truth will continue to do so throughout the ages, helping any and all who are interested in rising above the expediency of the day—and its pressures. For, facing certain death and knowing the heart of man, Christ prayed for all those who would come to Him in the future: "Sanctify them by the truth; your word is truth" (John 17:17).

Prayer and personal revelation
Knowing that He would be facing a criminal's gruesome death, Christ continued to pray until He, too, was sanctified, and His expectations were finally and painfully brought into harmony with His Father's purpose. "For God so loved the world. . . ." With His own disciples too tired and too frail to

care, He, literally sweating blood, broke through to God's love and uttered the words of His destiny: "Your will be done" (Matthew 26:42). "In the same way, the Spirit helps us in our weakness. We do not know what we ought to pray for, but the Spirit himself intercedes for us with groans that words cannot express. And he who searches our hearts knows the mind of the Spirit, because the Spirit intercedes for the saints in accordance with God's will" (Romans 8:26-27).

How many times I pleaded that God would change my destiny and the destiny of the country I loved! How many times I pleaded with Him to reveal the future, my destiny and America's, so that we could embrace it without the shame and humiliation we were experiencing. How many long quiet walks! How often I tuned out of a conversation, lost in thought . . . or, was it prayer? I just didn't know how to pray, faced with so much pain and disappointment. Who does?

But prayer is what makes us real before God. Honest. Authentic. Without it, we are little more than astrologers looking into a book in a vain attempt to predict the future, alchemists looking for the formula to change lead into gold.

But for the believer, prayer is the only authentic way to face pain. And in pain, there is only one authentic prayer. We see it throughout the Scriptures, from Job through the Prophets, and finally in the life of Christ and Paul. Whether it be a thorn in the flesh or a cross upon which the flesh of one man is to be crucified for all mankind, after all the begging and pleading for God to change His plan is done, we find humble acceptance of it . . . and the grace to obey. "Your will be done."

All the processes of God, His general and special revelations of Himself, are designed to bring us to that point of personal revelation. Complete trust is the essence of faith. To that extent, the Bible is the platform that launches us into the profoundly personal aspect of our faith: prayer. It prepares us for the struggle that is necessary for anyone who wants to encounter God. His manual was not given to us to reduce Him to a few basic principles so that we could become "smart enough" to live without Him. His creation, His book, and His Son teach us only one thing: the struggle is part of His plan. There is no crown without a cross. "Blessed is the man who perseveres under trial because when he has stood the test, he will receive the crown of life that God has promised to those who love him" (James 1:12).

I was heading home. My test was over—at least for the time being. During the ordeal, I had learned to study a different manual and to pray in its light. As I prayed, whether it was in the self-righteous anger of Job demanding that his circumstances change or the passionate plea of Paul or Christ humbly beseeching a loving Father, I realized that in the process something had changed, and profoundly so. I saw it all differently.

My heart and mind had been forced to comply with certain realities that had shattered something within me. Youthful optimism? Probably. Faith in America? I didn't think so, though it was still too soon to tell. I was too close to it. And so was the country. We needed time, space. I knew that I had been ushered into something bigger, and I was not yet comfortable with it.

It wasn't that I loved America less; it was simply that I now loved the Kingdom more—and its King! I had a new Father, a new home, and a new set of values, which had together changed the basic direction of my life. I wondered if this new perspective itself wasn't the "crown of life . . . promised to those who love him." For, as my freedom flight took off, in more ways than one, I had the assurance that I was truly on my way home.

In exchanging one world for another, I would soon be

back in the land animated by two of history's greatest gifts: the Constitution and a dream. Together they proclaimed a man and a woman's God-given right to seek after their own happiness as they defined it. But now, in light of the Kingdom, I also knew that this right would stay only as untarnished and noble as the men and women who embraced it. America would rise or fall on the quality of the individual American life. I wondered if we were still capable of uttering those prayerful words of destiny, "Your will be done."

Approaching America, I began to pray in thanksgiving and praise, but also in concerned petition, "Our Father, who art in heaven. . . ."

CHAPTER FOURTEEN
On Eagles' Wings

*"You . . . have seen . . . how I carried you on
eagles' wings and brought you to myself."*
(Exodus 19:4)

■

Homeward bound on the freedom flight—at last! It seemed
so unreal, so anticlimactic. On the plane I met an old buddy,
John, a fellow cadet from back at the Academy. Those years
now seemed like an eternity ago.

Because of the intensity of that environment, friendships were mostly just functional relationships. As energetic
cadets, we were too busy, too active, too caught up in it all to
really get to know one another. To us, it was more important
to get a job done, and perhaps cut an image in the process,
than it was to have a close friend. Everything we did was
unconsciously aimed at living up to something, some
expectation—becoming someone in someone else's eyes.
But whose? That, we didn't really seem to know. We'd been
too busy to ask ourselves, "Who are we living for, and why?"

I guess you could have called it an achievement syndrome. We dreamed of a life filled with multiple successes,

where results took precedence over all and people were only the means to a greater end. Self-actualization—that is, life on our terms. Up until the war, we had been typical young Americans. What else?

But now it was all different. Though I still wore the same uniform, and proudly so, the man coming home was not the same man who had left. Though there were still many unanswered questions, I knew that God had been faithful to His word—and to me. He had, in a deeper, more significant way, brought me to Himself, changing my perspective and challenging my values. I had grown in a myriad of ways I could not yet express. However, given the opportunity, I could overcome my reticence and share some of my more intimate observations on life if I felt the person listening to me could handle it. John could.

So when we found each other on the plane going home, each of us with his own brand of combat fatigue, we began to explore our perceptions and feelings about family, country, life, and, ultimately, God. The pressure was off. For us the war was over. Finally, there was nothing more to prove, nothing to lose. We just didn't have the energy to play the game anymore. Life had reduced us down to our real essence, and with the help of a cup of coffee, we were in the process of discovering each other's souls—as the freedom flight carried us home.

The soul

In the Scriptures, the soul is associated with the body, the self, the mind, the heart, the emotions, a person's *essence*. It's the sum total of his influence—who he is and what he does.

The soul of a man is found in what his name represents to those around him. It's the mood he creates when he walks into a room. There's a certain "fragrance" about him. That's why "a good name is better than fine perfume . . ." (Ecclesiastes 7:1). The soul relates to a person's character and the sum total of his influence. Being the product of his world view, a man's soul is shaped essentially by the example he has been following. It is the essence of who and what a man is—and why. It's all summarized in his name.

For example, when we say the names of Washington and Jefferson, feelings of admiration are evoked in the heart of an American as he reflects upon their contribution to the country. In spite of tremendous obstacles and their own human failings, these men are remembered for their personal sacrifices and the service they rendered to their generation and to posterity. Two hundred years later, our consciences continue to affirm the dignity that can be found in their example and message to their fellow man.

But, taking the idea one step further, let's discuss just one more name—the name that, according to Paul, is above all names (Philippians 2:9-11). It is a name that will outlive all others, not because He triumphed as Caesar had or was "successful" in the modern American sense of the word. He will be remembered because He incarnated the essence—the soul!—of this brief existence known as life in a way that no other person ever has or ever will. Jesus. The Christ!

It is the essence of His soul, His "fragrance," that should be the mark of the Christian (2 Corinthians 2:14-16). For, when the armies have stopped marching and the legislatures have ceased their debates, every knee shall bow and every tongue shall confess Jesus, who humbly lived among us to say and do all that was essential for life. "Love each other as I have loved you" (John 15:12). In this is our dignity and our being. Now, more than ever, the question for us all is Christ's own: "What good is it for a man to gain the whole world, yet forfeit his soul? Or what can a man give in exchange for his soul?" (Mark 8:36-37).

Rephrasing the question, we could simply ask: Who are our role models? Even if we pick the wrong ones, God loves us enough to set us free, and to turn our eyes toward the only perfect model: Jesus. To love purely and simply as He loved. Though occasionally the world does focus on this kind of love, for the most part it goes unnoticed. There is nothing attractive about a cross. Yet, as unappreciated as the Cross was at the time, human history was never more profoundly marked. As strange as God's will appeared to be, Jesus took the painful steps necessary to give Himself fully for that higher calling.

While He was being tempted in the desert, Jesus walked away from what this world had to offer—the power and prestige it could bring, the passions it could inflame, and the people and possessions it could buy. Later, as Jesus taught from His own experience, He referred to this process of making hard choices as "counting the cost" (Luke 14:25-33). Businessmen call it "opportunity cost." Choosing one option will cost you the opportunity that another option offers. It's simple logic.

But, put in a spiritual perspective, life's Author is forcing us to ask what true love demands. Will we pay the price? We have only so many hours in the day and only so much energy and emotion to give. And there are so many seemingly fulfilling options! But each of us must learn to ask, "What is my soul feeding on? Can I still walk away from a so-called golden opportunity in this fallen world in order to more fully respond to the truly golden opportunity of love? Just how far will I follow Jesus?"

Flying home that day from the war, perhaps these were the unspoken questions on my heart. John and I were both struck by how much the war had changed us. Before, we had known each other's dreams, hopes, and expectations. But now, in retrospect, they seemed so infantile in comparison to what we had seen and experienced.

For our eyes had been opened to the true meaning of the word sacrifice. Not that we had ourselves sacrificed that much or were now even ready to do so. Life had spared us that, at least for the moment. But we had both had that rare privilege of knowing those who had given all. Those who would never return. And their gesture had reduced us to humble admiration and silence. In their own way, they had literally demonstrated the meaning of Christ's words: "Greater love has no one than this, that he lay down his life for his friends" (John 15:13). However, because the country's mood was cynical and confused at the time, John and I openly wondered whether their sacrifice could ever go beyond the appreciation of just family—and the friends for whom they died.

As the plane landed, we both knew there was a good possibility we would never see each other again. However, we also knew that the aftermath of a war had fused our souls together. As we said goodbye, we knew we could understand each other. But we did not know if the country ever would. However, that too became one of the more unique aspects of what bonded us to each other and to the other veterans of our longest and most divisive war. Something had happened to us and the nation, and it was still too soon to say exactly what.

The memorial

It was the spring of '86. Fourteen years had passed since that fateful Easter in Vietnam. The sun was rising to a pink sky with a beauty surpassed only by the cherry blossoms surrounding a monument in the heart of the nation's capital. While I had been living in Europe, America had begun the healing process. The unveiling of the Vietnam Memorial led to a tearful expression of national reconciliation with its past. Veterans came to terms with their experience. Many cried—some bitterly. For most, however, the tears were in remembrance of lost friends, a lost youth—and what might have been.

Through parades, TV documentaries, and the analysis of the press, average citizens had finally begun to speculate on the meaning of it all. Why did it happen? What did we learn there? While America was going through this time of spiritual inventory, I had been too far away to be personally touched by it all. However, as I read the European commentary on the event, I saw just how much the nations of war-scarred Europe could understand their younger cousin as she sadly faced her symbol of inconsistency.

But now, having finally recrossed the ocean that had separated us too long, it was my turn. After a sleepless night, I, too, began my pilgrimage to the monument . . . and back to Nam!

In that war, I had been considered "mission essential personnel." I had spent a total of eighteen months in the theater of operations and, through those darker moments of my life, I had amassed a thousand hours of combat flying time in over two hundred missions. In the process, I had changed. I had lost some illusions—and some cherished friends. It was now time to pay my respects. But as I walked, I wondered how I would hold up, facing it all again.

Vacillating somewhere between anger and fear, I approached that manicured park filled with its imposing bright monuments to great men. Men I had read about all my life: Washington, Jefferson, and Lincoln. Men who had forged a great nation out of chaos by the force of their character and the clarity of their vision. Men who had sacrificed greatly for what they believed in, who had signed the orders of other men, usually younger, who did the same.

A mile away, across the Potomac River in Arlington

National Cemetery, stood the thousands of white marble monuments to those who had trusted in the dream. They had all given themselves for a hope, a vision, a dream called America, and, having paid the ultimate price, had wrought great victories and brought honor upon themselves and the nation. They were beloved by a country still young enough to believe in patriotism.

Now, however, in their midst was another monument. A dark one. A sobering ebony testimony to the men and dreams we had all lost in a different war. Vietnam.

After so many years, now I finally stood alone with that giant symbol . . . and my memories. Silenced by that hallowed ground, I reverently looked up the names of some friends in the register and began to note where they could be found among the fifty thousand so honored for their gift to the nation. I wept. They were not the bitter tears of anger, which I had feared would flow. The tears were those of a man who had found a soul mate. A long lost friend. Someone who could understand. For, there before me, etched into those dark marble pages of our history, were Scotty, Judd, Rusty, and the others. That dawn, alone with them again, I sighed the tear-filled sigh that speaks of rare moments that defy words . . . and I prayed. "Our Father, who art in heaven, hallowed be Thy name. . . ."

Thy kingdom come

As I stood there, I began to ask what this memorial had to say to a nation and to a lone veteran. It certainly was a tribute to the men who had gone—their heroism and their trust in the constitutional system that had sent them. In its own unique way, it stood for an America still committed to the propagation of those freedoms. It was also, however, a tribute to the families whose names are carved into that dark stone along with the loved ones they've lost. They, more than most, know the price of patriotism. And certainly they know how hollow tributes can be when paid by those who have not personally felt the weight of such sacrifice.

As I stood there, words escaped me. How could I express what those relationships had meant to me? How privileged I was to have known those men in spite of the war that had literally thrown us together, for better or worse. How do you say thanks to the guy who, over that late night cup of coffee, laughingly talked about everything and nothing, and then finally shared the silence of eternity? How do you say thanks to the fellow who shouted over the radios, "Break right!" just in time for you to avoid a clip of triple-A or a missile? How do you say thanks for the joke, dark as it was, that lifted the heaviness, even if it was just for the moment? And how do you say thanks for the few who, like yourself, felt the genuine need to pray, desperately pleading for a new King and a new Kingdom to reign on earth.

Standing there before them again to merely say "thanks" seemed such a futile gesture. Too little, too late. But in the same way, in light of their sacrifice, so was the monument. It was only a symbol. A gesture, which, like any gesture, is reserved for those whose eyes have been opened to its significance. How long I stood there humbled by its meaning, I can't say. But eventually as I stood there before the names of the men I loved, I came to attention and saluted one last time.

Thy will be done

However, before I turned to walk away, I realized it was finally time to share with anyone who would listen, for there was another lesson written into those dark marble tablets—one that has marked every combatant in every war throughout history. As the prophet says, "A voice says, 'Cry out.' And I said, 'What shall I cry?' 'All men are like grass, and all their glory is like the flowers of the field. The grass withers and the flowers fall, because the breath of the LORD blows on them. Surely the people are grass. The grass withers and the flowers fall, but the word of our God stands forever'" (Isaiah 40:6-8).

In his own poetic way, Isaiah is here reminding us all that the passage of time and its end point, death, are merely the "breath of God." For the most part, it blows gently, and by the second, minute, hour, and day, it gradually "withers" whatever is not wrought in eternity. For, as the mere petals of human accomplishment fall, that which is divine is brought into focus.

On occasion, however, the "breath of God" blows with all the force of a war's cyclone. According to the prophets, its purpose is to profoundly shock people into a more eternal perspective or to bring them back to the values they have abandoned. We simply do not ask the tough questions about the meaning of it all unless we are forced to. We will not ask about what's real, lasting, and worthy until our illusions have been exposed or destroyed by the reality of death, the breath of God. Judgment.

While still too young to fully appreciate its significance, I learned that when Caesar returned from his Gallic campaigns dragging the tribal chieftains behind him in chains, there was a young priest in the victor's chariot with him. While the crowd cheered the arrival of their new god, who was wearing the triumphal apparel reserved for the few singled out to contribute to the greater glory of Rome, the youth quietly but persistently whispered, "Remember that you are just a man."

"All men are like grass" is a prophet's way of saying the same thing. Though death should not dominate our thinking, its voice should certainly counsel us as we seek our own place in the sun, reminding us that we are only human and forcing us to ask, "What goal is worthy of a man's life?"

Just a generation after Julius Caesar's triumphal return, Jesus Christ stood condemned by that same Rome. It was Rome's "golden age." The Pax Romana. Much good had come out of the Roman Empire. East had met West, and commerce took place on paved roads freed of bandits. And all those roads led to Rome, the cultural and economic center of the civilized world. At that point in history, Roman citizenship seemed to be the key to all that was worthy in this life and Pontius Pilate's generation found its identity and dignity in all that was Roman.

However, Pilate also discovered that there were these stubborn Jews in Palestine and a carpenter raised in the tradition of their prophets who dared to believe that what was true for men was also true for nations. The breath of God continues to blow, and only that which is touched by the Divine will last. History itself has a hidden agenda, which Jesus so beautifully summarized in the words, "Thy will be done." For, according to Isaiah, "Surely the nations are like a drop in a bucket; they are regarded as dust on the scales; he weighs the islands as though they were fine dust. . . . Before him all the nations are as nothing; they are regarded by him as worthless and less than nothing. To whom, then, will you compare God? What image will you compare him to?" (Isaiah 40:15-18).

Here the prophet teaches us that as nations and their leaders come and go, God is behind it all. Sometimes gently, sometimes shockingly, He is calling a people to Himself and to the values of His Kingdom. Checking the excesses of men and nations by the excesses of other men and nations to bring about His plan, in His time, God is judging, purging history of its vanities. Breathing upon it. Forcing men to come to grips with His eternal agenda: love, as Christ loved. In the midst of it all, His breath can be felt, refining or inspiring a person and a people to live in light of His word, which, being

"God-breathed," will stand forever.

How long the Vietnam Memorial will stand no one can say, but in its own way it falls into harmony with that eternal theme. As I stood there, I realized deep within myself something about the nature of sacrifice and love. As young as my comrades had been, they would now be remembered for a sacrifice that should cause us all to ask: For whom are we willing to lay down our lives? This, I feel, is the monument's legacy to us. That is, in spite of it all, these young men had given everything. And I realized that in spite of it all, so should I. But, would I?

Staring into the cold marble darkness of that memorial, images of a life flashed across my mind. I saw a young idealist. Myself. I saw him leave the home he loved and the family he held dear to pursue an adventure. While still a cadet, he traveled through the Orient, "looking for something." Maybe to "find" himself. But he discovered only that a war awaited him there.

Returning to finish his final year at the Academy, he was filled with unanswered questions. Life. What was the meaning of it all? Something drove him on in his quest. From psychology to physics to philosophy, his mind and heart roamed the human archives "looking for something." Then, facing the war that his country no longer seemed to understand, he returned to the Bible his mother and father had spoken of so highly during his youth.

That Bible went with him into pilot training and, ultimately, into the war. Though some villages were saved, one in particular burned its way into his heart. Then, on another occasion, he saw a comrade begin to lose his sanity when he realized, "We're killing people!" Yet the missions continued. The pressure was on. "We had to stop them!" In trying to do so, that young idealist encountered the stone-cold silence of eternity. For, some of his friends had been

lost; others, captured. Still other downed pilots were counting on their comrades to rescue them.

So, these men risked it all, fighting desperately to save
their friends, facing the missiles and the guns of a determined
enemy that stood in their way. During those crucial weeks,
the struggling young idealist heard a scream over the radio:
"The chopper's going down!" The tragedy of it all. The
pathos. Duty.

Later, he called out to a crew caught in a spiral, only to
be answered by the silence of death. And those silent airwaves created waves of despair that a routine debriefing
could never dispel. War! There he was in the middle of it all,
still looking for something. No, some*one*. Where was God?!

And he waited. . . .

Finally, the silence was broken. There was a clear and
compelling message. Oh, how that Bible spoke! He searched
through that book night after night, day after day, in spite of
the pressure to prepare for another mission that might very
well be his last. In the process, he discovered God's revelation of Himself, and the importance of a man's conscience.
He saw afresh the Messiah who had stamped human history
for all time with the love of God—forgiveness! And in
newfound humility, he accepted that love, thus learning to
embrace God Himself, and the promised grace to face life as
he found it. He kept holding on to that grace until a freedom
flight brought him safely home. It was finally over.

But in another way, it had just begun.

Now, fourteen years had passed. How long I stood there
reliving it all, I cannot say. Time had illuminated those
bittersweet memories. Now I saw just how clearly God had
transformed my pain into perspective. All that I had been—
my training, my talent, and my idealistic world view—had to
be exhausted before I could see God and appreciate His plan.
In spite of it all, a divine encounter had taken place. Through

it all, an intimate dialogue had been established between an undeserving man and his Maker, with a power transcending even a war.

As it all flashed across my mind one more time, I could now understand how God had been faithful to His promise, day after day after day. He had, indeed, carried me on eagles' wings and had brought me to Himself. As I quietly walked away from that dark memorial, which now meant so much to me, I prayed yet again that God would grant me the grace to live in its light.